# *Letts*

# SUCCESS FOR SCHOOLS

# ICT

**2**

**TEACHING RESOURCES**

**PHOTOCOPIABLE**

## Sean O'Byrne • Chris Guy

Published by Letts Educational
The Chiswick Centre
414 Chiswick High Road
London W4 5TF

020 89963333
020 87428390
mail@lettsed.co.uk
www.letts-education.com

Letts Educational is part of the Granada Learning Group. Granada Learning is a division of Granada plc.

Text: © Sean O'Byrne and Chris Guy 2003

First published 2003

ISBN 1840859202

British Library Cataloguing in Publication Data

A catalogue record for this book is available from the British Library.

## Acknowledgements

The publishers would like to thank the following for permission to use copyright material. Every effort has been made to trace copyright holders and to obtain their permission for the use of copyright material. The author and publishers will gladly receive information enabling them to rectify any error or omission in subsequent editions.

The author and publishers are grateful to the following for permission to reproduce copyright material.

Microsoft Access®; Microsoft Excel®; Microsoft Internet Explorer®; Microsoft Notepad®; Microsoft Publisher®; Microsoft WordPad®; are registered trademarks of Microsoft Corporation. Screen shots (pp 58, 70, 73, 74, 75, 76, 81, 83) reprinted by permission from Microsoft Corporation. Dreamweaver® is a registered trademark of Macromedia, Inc.

Commissioned by Helen Clark

Project management by Vicky Butt

Editing by First Class Publishing Ltd

Cover design by Ken Vail Graphic Design, Cambridge

Internal design by  Ken Vail Graphic Design, Cambridge

Production by PDQ

Printed and bound by Ashford Colour Press

**Safety notice**

Whilst Letts has made all reasonable enquiries to ensure all the third party websites listed in this publication are suitable for KS3 students, Letts Educational does not endorse or approve the content of any such third party websites nor does it accept responsibility or liability for their content. Further, Letts makes no warranty or representation about anything contained in such third party websites referred to herein nor that their URLs will continue to be maintained, available and accessible and accepts no liability in connection with any suggestion or claim that any such third party website breaches any law or regulation or in any other way infringes on any of your rights. Also, you acknowledge that internet sites can change very quickly and Letts Educational accepts no responsibility or liability for any subsequent changes to the contents of any such third party websites, their URLs and/or any other online material.

Letts Educational strongly advises teachers, parents and/or guardians to access, review and monitor all such third party websites before directing students to them and also generally for schools actively to encourage parental supervision of students who are accessing the internet at home.

For government guidance on internet safety in schools, please see:

safety.ngfl.gov.uk/schools

For government advice on internet safety for parents, please see:

safety.ngfl.gov.uk/parents

# Curriculum and contents matching grid

| Lesson heading | Teacher page | Student page | Framework | SoW | NC |
|---|---|---|---|---|---|
| **Unit 1** | | | | | |
| Journey information | 4 | 4 | F2, F3 | Unit 8 | 1b, 1c |
| Information needs | 4 | 6 | F2 | Unit 8 | 1c, 3a, 5a |
| Displaying information | 5 | 8 | F1a, F1b | Unit 8 | 3a, 3b |
| Interactive systems or printed pages? | 6 | 10 | F2 | Unit 8 | 3a |
| Making a timetable spreadsheet | 6 | 12 | D4, D5 | Unit 8 | 3b |
| Planning a project | 7 | 14 | E1, E3 | Unit 8 | 2a |
| Designing the system | 8 | 16 | E3 | Unit 8 | 1c |
| Using flow charts | 9 | 18 | D3 | Unit 8 | 2d |
| Setting up the system | 9 | 20 | E4a, E4b | Unit 8 | 2a, 3a |
| Testing and evaluation | 10 | 22 | D7b, E3 | Unit 8 | 4a |
| Automatic data collection | 11 | 24 | D7a, D7b, D7c | Unit 8 | 2b |
| Computers in control | 11 | 26 | D8 | Unit 8 | 2b |
| Spreadsheet simulation | 12 | 28 | D7b | Unit 8 | 2c |
| **Unit 2** | | | | | |
| What are websites? | 13 | 30 | F1c | Unit 9 | 1b |
| Web tools | 13 | 32 | E4b, E5b | Unit 9 | 3a |
| Web page design features | 14 | 34 | E1, E2 | Unit 9 | 3a, 3b, 3c |
| An introduction to HTML | 15 | 36 | E6, E7 | Unit 9 | 3c |
| Some more HTML | 16 | 38 | E7 | Unit 9 | 3c |
| Using Microsoft *Word* to make a web page | 17 | 40 | D1b, E6, E7 | Unit 9 | 3b, 3c |
| Using *FrontPage* | 18 | 42 | E2 | Unit 9 | 3b, 3c |
| A school website | 18 | 44 | E1, E4a | Unit 9 | 3a, 3b |
| Mapping out the site | 19 | 46 | E6, E7 | Unit 9 | 3a, 3b |
| Building better pages | 20 | 48 | E5a | Unit 9 | 3b, 3c |
| Developing the site | 20 | 50 | E5b, E7 | Unit 9 | 3c, 4a |
| Testing and evaluating the site | 21 | 52 | D7b | Unit 9 | 3a, 3c |
| **Unit 3** | | | | | |
| Who holds data on me? | 22 | 54 | F7b, F7c | Unit 10 | 3a, 4b, 5d |
| The Data Protection Act | 22 | 56 | F7c | Unit 10 | 4b |
| Networks | 23 | 58 | F7a, F7b | Unit 10 | 1a 1b |
| Automatic data collection | 24 | 60 | F7a | Unit 10 | 4b 5d |
| EPOS and EFTPOS | 24 | 62 | F7a, F7b | Unit 10 | 4b, 5d |

Objectives are numbered consecutively as laid out in the *Framework for Teaching ICT Capability*.
F = Finding things out, D = Developing and making things happen, E = exchanging and sharing information

| Lesson heading | Teacher page | Student page | Framework | SoW | NC |
|---|---|---|---|---|---|
| **Unit 3** | | | | | |
| Loyalty cards | 25 | 64 | F7a | Unit 10 | 4a, 4b, 5d |
| Supermarket till receipts | 26 | 66 | F6a, F7a | Unit 10 | 1c 3b |
| Filtering and sorting data | 26 | 68 | F4 | Unit 10 | 2c 3a |
| Queries | 27 | 70 | F6b, F6c | Unit 10 | 3a, 5a |
| Mail merge | 28 | 72 | F7a, F7c | Unit 10 | 2a, 3a, 3b |
| **Unit 4** | | | | | |
| Effective web use | 28 | 74 | F1 | Unit 11 | 1a, 1b |
| Facts or opinions? | 29 | 76 | F1a, F1b | Unit 11 | 1b, 1c |
| Narrowing your search | 30 | 78 | F1b, F1c | Unit 11 | 1b, 4b, 4d |
| Search techniques | 30 | 80 | F4, F5 | Unit 11 | 1b, 1c, 5d |
| Producing graphs and statistics | 31 | 82 | D5 | Unit 11 | 2a, 2c |
| Data presentation formats | 32 | 84 | E5a | Unit 11 | 1b 2a |
| Fitness for purpose | 32 | 86 | E2 | Unit 11 | 3b |
| Further planning and DTP skills | 33 | 88 | E4a, E4b | Unit 11 | 3b |
| Making and evaluating the leaflet | 34 | 90 | E3, E5a, E5b | Unit 11 | 3b |
| **Unit 5** | | | | | |
| Project outline | 34 | 92 | F2, F3 | Unit 12 | 5c, 5d |
| Systems analysis | 35 | 94 | E4a, E4b | Unit 12 | 3c |
| Finance department | 35 | 96 | F3 | Unit 12 | 2c |
| Setting up the sheet | 36 | 98 | D1a | Unit 12 | 2c |
| Testing the spreadsheet | 37 | 100 | D4, D6 | Unit 12 | 1c |
| The bookings department | 37 | 102 | D7b | Unit 12 | 5c |
| Database implementation | 38 | 104 | F2, D3 | Unit 12 | 1c |
| Testing the database | 39 | 106 | F6a, D2 | Unit 12 | 1c |
| Mail merge | 39 | 108 | F4, F5 | Unit 12 | 3a 3b |
| Designing a logo | 40 | 110 | F7b | Unit 12 | 3a |
| Making a flyer | 40 | 112 | E5a | Unit 12 | 3a |
| An itinerary | 41 | 114 | E4a, E4b, E5a | Unit 12 | 3a, 3b |
| Information for school staff | 42 | 116 | E5a, E5b, D5 | Unit 12 | 3b |
| Starting a website | 42 | 118 | E1, E2 | Unit 12 | 3c |
| Planning and setting up the website | 43 | 120 | E3 | Unit 12 | 3a, 3c |
| Testing the website | 44 | 122 | E7 | Unit 12 | 3b, 3c |
| The final stages | 44 | 124 | D7b, E3 | Unit 12 | 4a, 4c |

Objectives are numbered consecutively as laid out in the *Framework for Teaching ICT Capability*.
F = Finding things out, D = Developing and making things happen, E = exchanging and sharing information

# Introduction

This book is the second in a series designed to provide a complete Key Stage 3 course in ICT. It follows the National Curriculum requirements, is matched to the QCA Scheme of Work and is modelled on the government's *Framework for Teaching ICT*. Any school that follows this course will automatically fulfil the teaching requirements as laid down in these documents.

## The Framework

The National Strategy *Framework for Teaching ICT Capability* is an ambitious attempt to raise the standards of ICT in schools. It recommends that all students at KS3 should be taught ICT as a discrete subject for at least one hour a week. It recognises that ICT is not as successfully delivered when solely taught by delegation as a cross-curricular exercise to other departments, although it has its place as a support to other subjects.

Inevitably, many teachers will be involved in the delivery of the Framework who are not specialists. The Letts *Success for Schools ICT* course is designed to help. It covers all the skills and knowledge required and is designed to be useable, more or less 'straight out of the box'. Experienced teachers of ICT will also benefit from the use of this course, as it removes much of the planning effort that would otherwise have to be expended.

*Success for Schools ICT* covers three overarching aims.

### 1 Skills

Students need to acquire a wide range of skills in the use of common software. This is absolutely essential if they are to be able to deploy ICT as a useful tool in other aspects of their work. It is recognised that many students, at all levels, still use software in a most rudimentary way, not taking advantage of all the labour-saving tricks that are available in all modern packages. For example, many are not aware of the time and effort that can be saved by something as simple as using keyboard shortcuts. These, and other basic approaches, are mentioned on many occasions throughout the course.

### 2 Application

It is of the most fundamental importance to realise where the use of ICT tools is appropriate and where it is not. Students following any ICT course will learn how ICT can save labour and also promote better results than using manual approaches. *Success for Schools ICT* provides many different contexts, both to do with schoolwork and also in pointing out ICT use in commercial scenarios. It is hoped that following this course will help students to see opportunities to use ICT tools in beneficial ways.

### 3 Knowledge

The speed of change in the world of ICT makes the teaching of it a unique challenge. However, ICT is still a subject, in many ways like any other. It has a body of knowledge, which has developed, albeit very quickly, over the 50 or so years that electronic computers have existed. It has its own jargon. Many users of computers complain about this, but knowledge of jargon is essential in any discipline to convey ideas and to describe the subject material. Consequently, terminology is firmly and unapologetically embedded in this course. Key terms are highlighted throughout the Student Book and a full glossary is provided. However, there is an ongoing expectation that students will build up their own glossary of terms.

## Teaching techniques

To make any subject interesting and enjoyable, most teachers want to use a variety of techniques. *Success for Schools ICT* tries to make this easy, by suggesting activities of a greatly varying nature. There are quizzes and puzzles to reinforce knowledge. Importantly, there are occasions when computers are *not* used. Having said that, it is advantageous and natural that, in a subject like this, use is made of the resources to produce most of the work. Most note taking should be done on a word processor and files retained as a portfolio. If the teacher so desires, representative work can be printed and held in a physical folder for assessment purposes.

## Resources

Certain assumptions have been made in terms of the resources available.

- *One computer per student (preferably networked)*
  This is because on many occasions, the students will need to practise and consolidate their own personal skills. On other occasions, group work is more natural.
- *A data projector*
  This is an invaluable aid. It is so easy to demonstrate techniques and ideas with a projector that all ICT classrooms ought, if possible, to have the use of one. It is also a very effective way of sharing the work of individuals with the whole group.
- *A general-purpose suite of Office software*
  This covers nearly all of the requirements. Indeed, modern software of this type contains enough power to support learning at KS3, and up to A-level and beyond.
- *A version of Logo*
  Most schools will have this already. It may be in use in the Maths Department.
- *Control and data logging*
  Many ICT departments do not possess a great deal of suitable hardware and software to handle these topics in a practical way. The course covers these topics in as practical a way as possible given limited resources. The Science and Technology departments are more likely to possess such resources and exposure to them would certainly be beneficial.

# How to use the Student Book

The Student Book is divided into five topic-based units. On the whole, each set of two pages will take about one 1-hour lesson with an able group. However, it is recognised that, in many cases, there is a lot to do and you will need to make your own judgements about how much a particular group can cover within a lesson. The book can be used in a flexible way and framework objectives checked in the contents grid. Many are covered more than once. Throughout the course, you will find the same pattern of headings used.

- *Aims*

   This section lists the major learning points for the lesson ahead. These are related to the Framework objectives listed on the contents grid at the front of the book (pages 2–3).
- *Starter*

   Following the 3-part lesson structure recommended by the Framework, each lesson opens with a starter activity.
- *Setting the scene*

   This feature reminds students of prior learning or alerts them to the topic for the next few lessons.
- *Fact panels*

   The development section of each lesson is delivered via a series of headed fact panels. Most contain a related activity to aid consolidation and deliver the practical elements of the course. Within the activities you will see these symbols:

   The activity requires use of a specified file from the CD accompanying these Teaching Resources.

   The activity requires use of a specified photocopiable worksheet. These are provided on pages 46–92 of these Teaching Resources.

- *Review*

   These are the plenary sections recommended by the Framework. Suitable homework questions are indicated by a satchel icon.

The design of *Success for Schools ICT* is highly visual. Many students and teachers will be familiar with this style, popularised by Letts's revision products. The colourful and non-sequential layout helps to make material accessible and memorable in the classroom.

## Curriculum matching

The contents grid at the front of the Student Book links each lesson to the relevant Framework objectives. The right-hand margin of each lesson also identifies whether the major thrust of the content relates to:

- Finding things out
- Developing ideas and making things happen
- Exchanging and sharing information

More detailed curriculum information is provided in these Teaching Resources (see next page).

## Differentiation

The Student Book contains material to provide ambitious work for the most able students. Clearly, many students will struggle to keep up. This can be accommodated within the Framework. It is not essential that all the activities in a given lesson are carried out. This can be taken into account when assessing the students – simply speaking, a portfolio of work from a less able student will contain less than that of one more able. Nonetheless, it is important to try and keep the pace brisk so that a wide variety of subject matter is encountered, even if the depth might not be all that would be achieved by higher ability students.

Suggestions for extension work are often given and the inclusion of such work in a portfolio will clearly mark out those for whom a higher assessment level is appropriate.

## Assessment

To aid in the assessment of a pupil's progress within the Framework, each lesson has been designed to cover elements of the Framework's objectives. The main focus is given at the start of the notes for each lesson. The assessment of a level will eventually be arrived at by examining a range of material once a portfolio has been accumulated.

## How to use these Teaching Resources

These Teaching Resources are essentially divided into two sections: lesson guidance for teaching staff and photocopiable resources for use in the classroom.

### Curriculum matching

The grid at the front of this book (pages iii–iv) matches the course content against the Framework, Scheme of Work and National Curriculum. This information is repeated in the teacher guidance for each lesson (pages 4–45 of this book) under the heading Curriculum link.

At the time of going to press, there are a number of sample teaching units available from the National Strategy. To ease planning, these units can be matched to the content of this course as follows.

| Sample teaching unit | Student book page | Teacher book page |
|---|---|---|
| Sample teaching unit 8.1 | 4 | 4 |
| Sample teaching unit 8.2 | 30 | 13 |
| Sample teaching unit 8.3 | 74 | 28 |
| Sample teaching unit 8.5 | 92 | 34 |

### Teacher's notes

Pages 4–45 of these Teaching Resources contain lesson notes following the heading structure of the Student Book. The lesson notes aim to provide additional useful information for the teacher: on conducting the practical activities; on preparing for each lesson; on the resources required; on likely outcomes; on differentiation, and more.

### Worksheets

Pages 46–92 of this book contain photocopiable worksheets linked to activities from the Student Book. Each sheet is linked to the corresponding page of the Student Book.

### CD

The enclosed CD accompanies both the student and teacher books. A full list of the contents of the CD is given below. These Teaching Resources are also provided in pdf form on the CD.

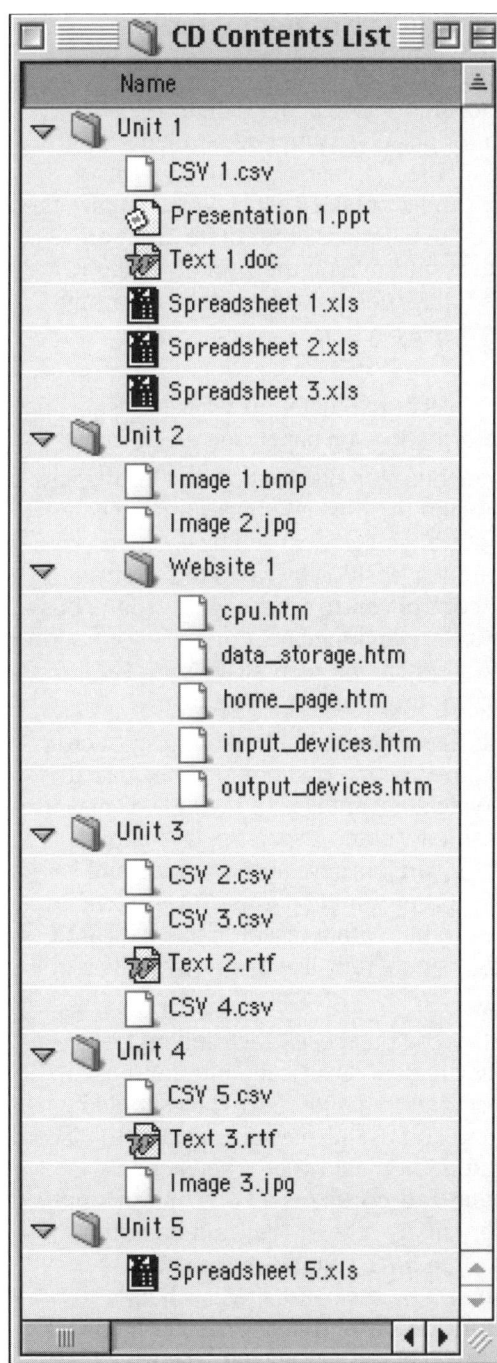

CD Contents List

```
Name
▽ Unit 1
     CSV 1.csv
     Presentation 1.ppt
     Text 1.doc
     Spreadsheet 1.xls
     Spreadsheet 2.xls
     Spreadsheet 3.xls
▽ Unit 2
     Image 1.bmp
     Image 2.jpg
   ▽ Website 1
        cpu.htm
        data_storage.htm
        home_page.htm
        input_devices.htm
        output_devices.htm
▽ Unit 3
     CSV 2.csv
     CSV 3.csv
     Text 2.rtf
     CSV 4.csv
▽ Unit 4
     CSV 5.csv
     Text 3.rtf
     Image 3.jpg
▽ Unit 5
     Spreadsheet 5.xls
```

# Journey information

## Curriculum link

**Framework coverage:** F2, F3

**SoW:** Unit 8

**NC:** 1b, 1c

**Prior learning:** Familiarity with looking up information on travel timetables would be of help. It is also expected that the students are familiar with searching for information on the Internet using search engines. For best progress, they should be able to do this independently, without too much guidance.

## Resources

- Access to the Internet
- Printed timetables

## Suggested web addresses

- **www.ul.ie/~infopolis/existing/annex_f/f12.htm**
- **www.nationalrail.co.uk/**
- **www.intolondon.com/jp**

## Lesson guidance

The theme for this lesson is the gathering of information for a specific purpose. Students will be exposed to a variety of methods whereby travel information can be obtained. They will compare the methods and should realise that there are more ways to collect information than simply using ICT. Later in this unit, students will produce their own information display systems.

### Starter

The starter looks at two different ways of displaying the same information: on paper and electronically.

The electronic bus stop display has an LED display that shows when the next few buses are expected. It makes use of transmitters carried by each bus, which signal their position by radio to a control centre. The control centre sends signals to the bus stop displays by telephone line. Further information about this system can be seen at **www.ul.ie/~infopolis/existing/annex_f/f12.htm**

The students are asked to think about how such a system compares with a traditional paper-based timetable. Typical advantages of the LED display are immediacy and accuracy. Paper displays allow passengers to plan journeys further ahead and compare more routes and options. The students may be interested to know that research has indicated that passengers generally like displays of this sort.

### Development

The students work on specific fact-finding tasks. In *Activity 1*, they look at specifically Internet-based resources for planning a journey. They should be encouraged to find useful sites quickly and to discard any sites that do not lead where they need. **www.nationalrail.co.uk/** is an obvious site, but there are very many others. The train operating companies often have suitable information and there are many specialist sites such as **www.intolondon.com/jp** for particular areas. The students should set out exactly why the sites they

have chosen are useful to them. They could consider issues such as starting points and destinations and ease of use.

*Activity 2* checks that the students have some 'traditional' timetable interpretation skills. Many students will not have experience of this sort of planning and a look at the practicalities of journey planning is a prerequisite for later developments.

*Activity 3* sets a specific journey-planning task so that students can see that there are several ways of interrogating the online timetables to arrange a journey so that they arrive in good time. Make time for a brief discussion about how the times given may still be unreliable. UK schools will be only too aware that many trains do not run to timetable or are cancelled at the last minute!

*Activity 4* brings *Activity 1* into more focus. Having looked at finding out something quite specific, students now try a specific enquiry with different providers. An additional benefit of this exercise is to set the students thinking about what makes a usable information system and how differently designed websites can provide different experiences and utility value to users.

### Review

Make quite specific points about difficulties in finding out what you need to know. This should help students later in the unit when they are making their own systems.

### Homework

The homework is preparation for the next lesson. The students should realise that, even when a journey has been planned, there may still be unforeseen circumstances that could affect these plans on the day of travel.

## Differentiation

Students who work quickly could plan a different or a more complex journey. One involving more than one mode of transport could provide further useful work. They could also consider producing a brief guide to others on how to find travel information as efficiently as possible.

# Information needs

## Curriculum link

**Framework coverage:** F2

**SoW:** Unit 8

**NC:** 1c, 3a, 5a

**Prior learning:** Previous lesson in this unit

## Resources

- Word-processing software
- Worksheet 1

## Lesson guidance

This lesson further develops the thought processes that will lead to the production of an information system. Issues such as what to display and how to display it are covered. From their work in the previous lesson, some students will now be aware that there is a great deal of variation in how information is displayed and that this can have a real impact on the usability of an information system.

### Starter

Using *Worksheet 1*, students are asked to consider features that make the display effective, such as shading, layout and the number of items displayed.

### Development

*Activity 1* focuses attention on breaking down the information that might be needed in planning a journey. A mind map in the Student Book provides some clues but encourage students to range beyond the ideas given. Some students might start to see the commercial possibilities of providing services that bring information together in one place. This exercise can be carried out on an individual basis.

*Activity 2* makes students think about a wide range of information types. This is a recurring theme throughout KS3 and the students should be encouraged to go beyond the list provided. Other examples of giving information include traffic lights, LEDs on computer equipment and Braille. In the activity, the students need to decide which elements are needed for the purpose. Take this opportunity to introduce or revise the term 'multimedia' and encourage students to add it to their glossary (if they have one).

Computers are not likely to completely supplant paper-based information systems. In *Activity 3*, the students are asked to consider why people often still prefer paper systems. Many issues could be raised, such as portability and visual comfort.

The issue of public computer systems is explored next. Many people are unaware that computer systems, possibly driven by an ordinary PC, are behind some of the impressive looking displays seen in public places. Sometimes, for example, displays such as flight departures at airports show the dreaded Windows 'blue screen' when there has been a software failure. The Internet continues to grow as the fastest means of informing the public and *Activity 4* asks the students to reflect on whether there is still a place for alternatives.

### Review

The issue of usability should be the main focus of this lesson, so remind students that the design of a user-friendly user interface is one of the great difficulties in software development, and the subject of much extensive and expensive research.

### Homework

Students should work individually to produce a better user interface than the one shown in the Student Book.

## Differentiation

There are many public information systems that attempt to keep people up to date. Students who are working quickly can list such situations and suggest the origin of the incoming data.

# Displaying information

## Curriculum link

**Framework coverage:** F1a, F1b
**SoW:** Unit 8
**NC:** 3a, 3b
**Prior learning:** Previous lessons in this unit

## Resources

- Word-processing software
- Spreadsheet software
- Worksheet 2

## Lesson guidance

This lesson covers a variety of ways that tabulated data can be set out clearly. Emphasise the importance of keeping to a design brief so as to keep the client satisfied.

### Starter

It is important that opportunities are taken throughout KS3 to reinforce the learning of correct terminology. The wordsearch on *Worksheet 2* contains terms that relate to presentation of information.

### Development

By Year 8, students are well acquainted with the use of various formatting techniques. Often, they think of formatting as a largely aesthetic procedure, but this lesson should demonstrate that there is great utility value to be had in the careful use of such effects as bold, italic and shading. The students look at an example timetable to see how different presentation techniques have important practical value in the special case of a timetable. *Activity 1* is designed to concentrate their minds on this aspect of presenting information.

Making the best use of tables is often a neglected skill with otherwise sophisticated word processor users. Tables are so useful and versatile that it is worth incorporating them into a variety of situations. *Activity 2* presents students with one method for inserting a table.

In *Activity 3*, the students start to plan a timetable document. They are given a straightforward design brief to produce a pocket timetable and the activity is designed to concentrate their minds on exactly what has to be done. Point out to students that they cannot be allowed the freedom they may have enjoyed with other exercises because, as in real-life, there are always tight constraints on the production of various artefacts.

Often, it is more convenient to produce a tabulated document using a spreadsheet rather than a word-processed table. Stress to students the great advantages that can be gained by thinking of a spreadsheet as a text layout tool as well as a calculating resource. *Activity 4* explores this possibility and directs the students to use a spreadsheet to make their timetable.

### Review

Students should reflect on any difficulties that they might have encountered. The use of the spreadsheet might have posed certain formatting problems, e.g. in adjusting column width and alignment. Check that the students understand the 24-hour clock, and discuss any issues concerning the setting of time format in the cells and whether to use the 24-hour clock. Ask for comments on the pros and cons of using a word processor or a spreadsheet for their timetable.

### Homework

Students review their own work and this serves to reinforce the software skills that were covered in the practical activities.

## Differentiation

More able students could try to use formulae to work out the times of intermediate stops on the journeys.

# Interactive systems or printed pages?

10 | 11

## Curriculum link

**Framework coverage:** F2

**SoW:** Unit 8

**NC:** 3a

**Prior learning:** Previous lessons in this unit coupled with a knowledge of hardware terms.

## Resources

● Word-processing software
● Access to the Internet
● Worksheet 3

## Suggested web addresses

● **www.nationalrail.co.uk/**
● **www.virgintrains.co.uk/**
● **www.centraltrains.co.uk/**

## Lesson guidance

This lesson is concerned with interactive event-driven systems in keeping with most modern computer systems.

It contains some significant computing concepts that should be given considerable emphasis.

### Starter

Using *Worksheet 3*, students complete a wordsearch quiz. This reminds them of various items of computer hardware and such reinforcement should help them to accumulate the necessary 'jargon' for further development and for the possibility of tests.

### Development

*Activity 1* asks the students to look around their school to see how much use is still made of the printed word and image. There will always be a place for printed information. However, electronic displays are becoming ever more common; they are easy to update and can give people better

information about all sorts of services. Discuss how people can become angry when things go wrong, e.g. when a train does not arrive on time and the passengers do not know the reason why it is late or when it might arrive. Updated information can help our tempers!

*Activity 2* asks the students to think widely about situations where electronic displays are to be found: such as car dashboards; domestic electronic goods; and many different transport applications, e.g. the illuminated signs above motorways that warn of problems ahead.

The displays considered so far have been passive – someone provides the information on them and other people read them. Increasingly, the interactivity seen in event-driven programs is appearing in public systems. Most of all, this is apparent on the Internet, where many websites are now interactive. *Activity 3* focuses on just one example of an interactive page. Encourage students to think about how interactivity increases the utility value of a display and some of the ways in which this can be achieved.

*Activity 4* names the parts according to *Windows* conventions; encourage students to learn some of the terminology and how the objects mentioned can be put to practical use.

### Review

The students should be guided to the suggested websites. All require interaction.

### Homework

Ask students to put to work the material they have covered in the lesson. It could lead to a quite sophisticated piece of design work from the better students. This homework is needed for the Starter activity in the lesson 'Planning a project'.

## Differentiation

The more aware students can add to their designs the names of the *Windows* objects that they would use on the information point. They might also consider what data would need to be collected to make this work.

# Making a timetable spreadsheet

12 | 13

## Curriculum link

**Framework coverage:** D4, D5

**SoW:** Unit 8

**NC:** 3b

**Prior learning:** Basic spreadsheet operations

## Resources

● Spreadsheet software
● CD: CSV 1

## Lesson guidance

The students have already used a spreadsheet to make a train timetable. In this lesson, they formally work through some of the issues that may have presented difficulty before.

### Starter
The starter focuses students' thinking on the wide variety of data that we work with in our daily lives and highlights the need for processing that data. Encourage students to think clearly about processing needs; it will help them to make the right choices in a wide variety of ICT activities in the future.

### Development
The students have already started to think about some less obvious ways of using spreadsheets. Here, in *Activity 1*, the process is extended; students are asked to suggest data sets that could be manipulated by a spreadsheet. It is intended that these may, but do not necessarily have to involve calculations.

Follow this with a brief consideration of formatting cells. Draw attention to the way in which the times are displayed in the Student Book; students need to know how to produce this effect. In some versions of *Excel*, a time entered as 09:15 (with a colon) will be recognised by the software as a time value, and can be processed accordingly. Entering 09.15 (i.e. with a decimal point) will be interpreted as a number and, to display it as a time, the Format – Cell feature will need to be used to amend the format so that processing is possible.

In *Activity 2*, students import the prepared, *CSV 1*, file and make sure that the format is correct.

*Activity 3* centres around the facility within a spreadsheet to perform calculations on time values. This will not work unless the data are correctly formatted to time.

*Activity 4* uses familiar spreadsheet functions to find maximum and minimum journey times. Encourage students to check that their answers are reasonable, because it is easy to make mistakes.

### Review
This lesson has only scratched the surface of the formatting power of modern spreadsheets. Use this review time to point students in the direction of many other possibilities. Using their spreadsheet software, encourage students to look at what is available under the Format – Cell menu item.

### Homework
Tabular displays should be made attractive and easy to read. This is possible using spreadsheet features. For this homework, students are encouraged to think about how to improve the readability of tabulated information, e.g. using shading and colouring, by adjusting cell sizes, setting alignments and including borders.

## Differentiation
Students who are working quickly can explore other spreadsheet functions to produce journey statistics. They can also use drawing tools to highlight certain parts of the timetable.

# Planning a project

## Curriculum link
**Framework coverage:** E1, E3
**SoW:** Unit 8
**NC:** 2a
**Prior learning:** Previous lessons in this unit

## Resources
- Word-processing software
- Access to the Internet

## Suggested web addresses
- www.jobserve.co.uk

## Lesson guidance
As the students progress through their ICT work, there will be increased emphasis on placing their skills into a context. The contexts become more ambitious and start to resemble real-life projects in which many skills have to be deployed. This lesson leads into such a multi-skilled project and introduces some of the formal methodology that is used in project management and systems analysis. This will stand the students in good stead if they later follow a GCSE course in ICT.

### Starter
Students need to refer to the material produced for homework in the lesson 'Interactive systems or printed pages?'. By looking at the work of others and giving constructive criticism, they have an opportunity to consider further aspects of good user interface design.

### Development
The standard stages of the system life cycle are briefly defined here, and this gives a simple view of what happens where – which should be helpful to KS4 students who often have needless difficulties with this. Some of the stages are 'traditionally' dealt with by systems analysis, although there is often a blurring of roles, especially in smaller project teams. Take this opportunity to point out that systems analysis is still a promising employment option; maybe some of the students might eventually want to move in that direction! *Activity 1* can therefore be viewed as an early piece of careers information as well as an object of study. Encourage students to visit online recruitment sites such as **www.jobserve.co.uk** to find out the details required.

Students then need to look at the problem: as in any ICT project, they need to see what is going wrong at the moment and how a computer-based solution might be of use. For *Activity 2*, encourage students to pay due regard to the language to be used when putting forward a business proposition.

Students often have problems identifying what needs to be done to analyse a task. Understanding the requirements of the new system is a necessary part of this process, so encourage students to think in bullet points. This will make it easier to keep track of their progress with the project. For *Activity 3*, students need to recognise the subtle difference between a requirement and an objective. This analogy may help: a requirement of a Formula 1 racing team is to win the race; one objective could be to perform a pit stop in under 8 seconds. It is the difference between 'what' and 'how'. In real life, it is the 'how' that the programmers can work on.

Students then look at these objectives in more detail. For *Activity 4*, students need to identify the input and output for their project. Input and output requirements are fundamental to the design of any system – computer or otherwise. Use brief discussions of non-IT systems such as a kitchen to put this in perspective: the input is the ingredients and the output, after processing, is a meal. Encourage students to look at the output first; it can be easier to identify what is wanted from the system, and then the input becomes a necessity to produce the required output.

### Review

Use this opportunity, just as in a real-life project planning meeting, to bring together all the thoughts and ideas that students have individually worked on in these activities. Reinforce what has happened so far, and encourage the use of correct terminology as far as possible.

### Homework

Encourage students to focus on customer satisfaction for their letter to the station manager.

## Differentiation

More able students could apply the requirements of problem analysis to other scenarios, such as the organisation of a social event, and consider – briefly at this stage – the inputs and outputs required.

# Designing the system 16 17

## Curriculum link

**Framework coverage:** E3
**SoW:** Unit 8
**NC:** 1c
**Prior learning:** Previous lessons in this unit

## Resources
- Word-processing software
- Worksheet 4
- Access to the internet

## Suggested web addresses
- **www.melair.com.au/flight_info/index.asp**

## Lesson guidance

This and the next lesson focus on designing parts of the information system, along with some stages that traditionally belong in the analysis stage. Students should be made aware that this is the design section and that it is concerned with planning the small details that can be put to use when making it all happen in reality (the implementation).

### Starter

To consider aesthetics, and more importantly, functionality, students are asked to think about how their computer desktop is set out and how this may make it easy to use. Give the discussion some historical background, and tell students how, with the earliest computers, users had to learn and then type in lots of commands to make the computers do what was intended. Indeed, programmers had to set switches manually or make holes in paper tape to issue instructions. The production of an easy-to-use interface has brought computing to everyone and the students should realise just how critical user friendliness is and how an entire industry has been based on this.

### Development

The students grapple with moving their information system along. The tasks set in *Activity 1* are often carried out in the analysis phase, but as the students are performing the whole task from start to finish, there are no division of labour issues here. The students can work individually or in pairs, but they should all appreciate the basic questions to be answered at this point.

Take the opportunity to emphasise that computers process data but do not care what they mean. It is up to humans to place meaning on what a computer outputs.

*Activity 2* focuses attention on how to make the output mean something to the users of the system. The students can again work individually or in pairs.

Some basic rules for making an interactive system look good and easy to use are then explored. A typically well-produced and well-known website is that of the BBC. It is often a good choice when wanting to demonstrate good practice in web design, secure in the knowledge that the content will be reliable and safe.

*Activity 3* asks the students to carefully analyse how the BBC creates an easy-to-see website.

For an information system such as a website or a public display to be useful, it must be kept up to date and, nowadays, people expect immediacy from such systems. *Activity 4* asks the students to consider ways that this might be achieved; in particular, how the updated information could be gathered and input into the system.

### Review

Consider the issues of a usable interface and encourage students to apply what they have learned to their own task.

### Homework

*Worksheet 4* is given to the students to help them to decide the essential components that they will need in their system.

## Differentiation

The issue of immediacy can be explored further by visiting one of the many websites that now give up-to-the-minute information about real-time events.

For example, most airports have live updates of arrivals and departures: **www.melair.com.au/flight_info/index.asp** is just one example. Students could make some comments on how such sites might be updated.

# Using flow charts

18 | 19

## Curriculum link
**Framework coverage:** D3
**SoW:** Unit 8
**NC:** 2d
**Prior learning:** Previous lessons in this unit, reasonable word-processing skills

## Resources
- Word-processing software, e.g. Microsoft *Word*
- Worksheet 5
- Worksheet 6

## Lesson guidance
This lesson concentrates on more standard ways of planning a project. Early exposure to such practices will help the students later on in planning a variety of other projects. Ensure that students use the correct symbols and put the right text into the boxes. These are the basic rules:
- A process box will contain a verb.
- A decision box will contain a question or test.
There are various diagrammatic ways of detailing a system. This lesson looks at process or algorithm flow charts and other planning aids, but not system flow charts.

### Starter
Students should work on *Worksheet 5*, preferably on an individual basis. They need to order the actions using the outline flow chart, and it is important that they grasp the idea of sequencing and the use of process boxes. Make students aware that each step is an action, i.e. contains a verb, as they complete each process box.

### Development
The students now put together the components of their information system, using standard process/program flow chart symbols. This activity should be carried out on paper and if students work in pairs, they can help each other. *Activity 1* uses *Worksheet 6* which contains start and finish symbols, process boxes and decision boxes. Tell students that a decision box contains a test; in this case, the test is 'Has a button been pressed?'. They are making decisions as a result of button-press events. Tell students that, typically, there is one input to a decision box and two outputs, one for 'yes' and one for 'no' as shown here:

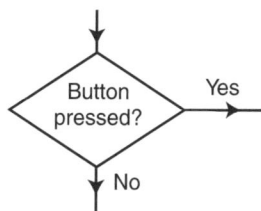

For *Activity 2*, students find out how easy it is to make flow charts that look good using the Microsoft *Word* drawing tools. The Student Book contains the basic instructions on how to do this, but remind students that right clicking on a shape brings up a pop-up window with various formatting actions. In particular, the Add text option is an essential feature for constructing flow charts. Encourage students to group the images into a single image, by shift-clicking on each symbol and selecting Draw – Group; then the finished flow chart will remain intact during any later editing.

An overview is needed, so, in *Activity 3*, students see a convenient way of planning the whole system. A tree diagram like this is useful because it can lead directly to the individual components of the final system such as pages or files. Encourage students to use the drawing tools of the word processor to make this diagram, and to consider landscape orientation if necessary.

For the train information you could invent a short list of three or four departure and arrival times. More able students could look up real times suitable for their nearest mainline station.

You may prefer to use the Microsoft Organisation Chart for this activity. If this is installed with *Word*, it is obtainable from the Insert – Object menu sequence.

### Review
Take this opportunity for further practice in flowcharting as a group activity.

### Homework
The project is moved forward in the homework by the production of some screen sketches.

## Differentiation
There is so much to do in this lesson that it is unlikely that all students will be able to follow all the possible ideas for formatting the diagrams. It is a good opportunity for assessment by outcome.

# Setting up the system

20 | 21

## Curriculum link
**Framework coverage:** E4a, E4b
**SoW:** Unit 8
**NC:** 2a, 3a
**Prior learning:** Previous lessons in this unit, *PowerPoint* skills

## Resources
- Word-processing software
- Presentation software
- Worksheet 7
- CD: Text 1
- CD: Presentation 1

## Lesson guidance
This lesson starts the actual implementation of the information system. It includes software choices and spends much time on developing practical skills.

### Starter

The starter crossword puzzle, on *Worksheet 7*, revises some of the terminology associated with system development. Make time for a quick revision of the meanings of the words and suggest that students add these terms to their glossaries.

### Development

*Word* can be used to produce some simple hypertext links. In *Activity 1*, the file *Text 1* shows such links in use. By asking students to adapt the file, they learn how to make the links. Students may use the hyperlink button on the toolbar, or they can use the Insert – Hyperlink menu sequence. Either will bring up a dialogue box where they can navigate to the target page via the Place in this document button.

Note that, while it is possible to use *Word* to make web pages by saving a document as a web page, for many reasons, it is not a good way forward. For example, the HTML code produced is messy and very difficult to edit.

To make the functioning information system required for this project, presentation software such as Microsoft *PowerPoint* has advantages over *Word*. Notably, this is because it is intended to be screen-based rather than on paper. *Activity 2* looks at a simple presentation along the lines of what is required. It is supplied on the file *Presentation 1*. This is intended to be a short session in which students can think about what they are about to do and produce some ideas.

In *Activity 3*, the students pull everything together that they need; this should show them how many separate resources are required for any project, quite apart from the hardware and the software.

### Review

Look at the practicalities of what the students have done and draw their attention to how they have solved any problems. Later project work often requires students to document the development process and indicate how decisions were made in response to problems.

### Homework

This encourages more thought about why hyperlinks are so useful. The students are asked to consider how they can help the reader.

## Differentiation

The more able students will have planned this work more meticulously than others. Again, there is an opportunity for assessment based on the degree of forethought that has gone into the system. More able students might reflect on the benefits of planning an exercise like this rather than jumping straight in and producing it.

# Testing and evaluation

22 23

## Curriculum link

**Framework coverage:** D7b, E3
**SoW:** Unit 8
**NC:** 4a
**Prior learning:** Previous lessons in this unit

## Resources

- Word-processing software
- Presentation software

## Lesson guidance

The normal progress through a project is continued here and the importance of testing is introduced. Discuss the fact that bad systems can be, at best, annoying to a user and, at worst, can lead to disasters and bankruptcy.

### Starter

Testing is purposeless unless there are performance criteria to judge against. In the starter, students look at the success criteria for this system, such as 'easy to read', 'quick response times', 'the links go to the right places' and 'the information is up to date'.

### Development

The above ideas for criteria and more are itemised in the Student Book. For *Activity 1*, students test each other's systems. Stress the need for testing to be done by someone else. Testing your own work is all well and good, but someone else will be less inclined to forgive inadequacies. The real purpose of testing a system is not just to 'see if it works'. Rather, it is to try and break it! Ask students to take this somewhat hostile approach so as to show the way forward for improvements.

All systems require documentation. The Student Book describes the two types of documentation produced – for the user and for anyone who might have to maintain the system. Obviously, a public information system should not require a full-blown manual for members of the public to read. However, in *Activity 2*, the students are asked to provide a very simple equivalent appropriate to this situation.

Finally: evaluation. Emphasise that this is not merely something annoying that teachers ask students to put into projects to fill the time! There is a real-life reason for this. Any commercial system will be evaluated throughout its life so that improvements can be made and thus it always fulfils its primary business purpose. *Activity 3* focuses on this.

*Activity 4* revises the system's life cycle. Check that the students' definitions are correct.

### Review

The stages of system development are reviewed here, so as to look forward to any future tests that the students will take. It also reinforces that ICT is a subject with its own disciplines and terminology, and not just an enabling tool for other activities.

### Homework

Self-evaluation is the theme of the homework; it is an easy extension to the peer evaluation of *Activity 3*.

### Differentiation

The more able students could go back to their original performance criteria and match these up with their evaluations, point by point.

# Automatic data collection

24 25

## Curriculum link

**Framework coverage:** D7a, D7b, D7c
**SoW:** Unit 8
**NC:** 2b
**Prior learning:** Year 7 work on automatic data collection (D5: Book 1 pp.108, 110, 116) and control (D5, D5a, D5b: Book 1 pp. 102, 108) and previous lessons in this unit

## Resources

● Access to the Internet
● Word-processing software

## Lesson guidance

The Year 7 work included material on data sensing and computer control. The focus here is to apply the principles from the earlier work to the practical problems of a public information system. The railway theme is continued.

### Starter

Revision of sensors is suggested for the starter activity. If the students have encountered the use of sensors in science work, the list should include such items as pressure pads, light sensors, thermistors, pH sensors, magnetic sensors as well as many others. The students ought to be able to think about many real-life situations where sensors are used.

### Development

Live updates of train movements for public displays can be achieved by tracking where the trains are at any moment. Unfortunately the displays at many big stations contain lots of entries where 'time expected' is certainly not the same as 'time due'! The collection of data to allow such live (and frustrating) updates can be by various methods, such as mobile telephones and signal box communications, but some automation is possible.

*Activity 1* shows live train information from any UK station.

*Activity 2* revisits the flow charting material by asking students to create a flow chart that could illustrate a tracking system.

The next lesson, *Computers in control,* looks at some issues about human involvement in railway operation. Use this opportunity to take a wider look at how computer systems can be of great benefit, but also to look at the need for a human overview. Accidents still occur despite increasingly

sophisticated systems and, often, human behaviour is at fault. For *Activity 3,* students look critically at how IT systems can help in this situation.

*Activity 4* looks at another way in which data that has been collected automatically can be used for statistical purposes. Some students might like to speculate on how such data might be used to mislead rather than illuminate. The activity is best suited to individual or pair work and should be word-processed.

### Review

This is a little straightforward revision, using the technique of supplying questions to answers rather than the other way round. The session could be used to update the students' glossaries.

### Homework

The homework is a fairly standard question about sensors, but the students may not have considered it before. They should think about what are the alternatives to sensors as they make their comparisons.

## Differentiation

*Activity 2* could be extended to include other factors by more able students. For example, a way of identifying the train as it passes a sensor could be included. Students could speculate on how this might be achieved.

Also, *Activity 3* could be extended to look at how computer systems contribute to safety in other situations such as air traffic control.

# Computers in control

26 27

## Curriculum link

**Framework coverage:** D8
**SoW:** Unit 8
**NC:** 2b
**Prior learning:** None

## Resources

● Spreadsheet software
● CD: Spreadsheet 1

## Lesson guidance

This lesson takes the issue of computer control rather further than in Year 7. The students look at basic computer logic so as to further understand how computers can control devices. The material goes a little beyond what might normally be expected at this stage, but it is basically very simple and most students can cope with it. More able students will enjoy mastering a few fundamental concepts.

### Starter

In this whole class activity students brainstorm a few ideas about computer-controlled devices at a train station. They ought to suggest ticket machines, information systems as covered in this unit, telephone systems, signalling, security gates and air conditioning (some stations have this!). There are plenty of things that ought to be computer controlled but are not.

### Development

The fundamental bi-stable technology of computers is mentioned here. The students might like to know that computers are so reliable because of the basic simplicity of the on-off principle and how it is easier to make reliable components based on this than on older analogue technologies.

In *Activity 1*– best as a whole class activity – students ought to be able to think of a few bi-stable devices such as light switches, doorbells, car horn, vacuum cleaner or indeed anything that is either 'on' or 'off' but never 'in between'.

The ticket machine panel is concerned with a little bit of computing theory in the sense of using variables. *Activity 2* requires the use of the file *Spreadsheet 1*. This is a straightforward demonstration of how a spreadsheet can be set up to make decisions and this can illustrate how a computer can control a device such as a ticket machine.

The students must click 'enable macros' when loading this file for it to work. They enter values for the coins inserted just as with a real ticket machine and press the button for the ticket when ready. They should enter some wrong data to see some error checking. This is an unusually kind ticket machine as it rejects excessive money input as well as insufficient! The activity asks the students to draw up a truth table: the normal AND truth table. The students should at least be able to work out that only one combination of conditions will give a ticket.

The same AND truth table applies to the next example in the *Ticket barrier sensors* panel. In *Activity 3*, students complete this. Emphasise the inherent simplicity behind computer control to the students, and how complex control systems are just lots and lots of simple systems like these, combined.

In the panel *The IF function and validation*, the students can see how the sheet is set up with validation rules to allow only certain coins to be accepted. It may be necessary to unprotect the sheet before the validation option can be explored. (Tools – Protection – Unprotect workbook). *Activity 4* asks students to look at the validation set up. They could also list some other possibilities offered by such validation mechanisms.

### Review

The review is another test of understanding by means of supplying questions to go with answers.

### Homework

This speculative piece allows students to let their imaginations run, but also to think about some practical realities. More able students will think of several human issues that give an opportunity for assessment.

### Differentiation

More able students should certainly look at the contents of cells B2, C2 and D2 to try to understand how the 'ticket machine' works. They could write a prose explanation of it.

They may want to alter the spreadsheet to allow it to accept overpayment. This can simply be achieved by changing the formula in cell B2 from =IF(A2=40,TRUE,FALSE) to =IF(A2>=40,TRUE,FALSE).

If they wanted to see the complete picture, they should look at the simple macros that lie behind the two command buttons as well. (Tools – Macro – Macros – (select a macro) – Edit). More able students should have no difficulty in understanding this simple code.

# Spreadsheet simulation

28 | 29

## Curriculum link

**Framework coverage:** D7b
**SoW:** Unit 8
**NC:** 2c
**Prior learning:** Previous work with spreadsheets

## Resources

- Spreadsheet software
- CD: Spreadsheet 2
- CD: Spreadsheet 3

## Lesson guidance

The lesson looks at simulations and distinguishes these from modelling. These two terms are often confused. Spreadsheets make it convenient to produce models and they also have features that can turn the models into simulations. Some further features of spreadsheets are also considered.

### Starter

It is always a good idea to think beyond the technicalities of ICT systems and look at the implications. Tell the class that there will always be differences in opinion as to the rights and wrongs of innovation. The previous homework was speculative. The starter gives an opportunity to see how many ideas and concepts are shared and how many are unique to one person.

### Development

Make students aware of why simulations are so useful. Discuss also some issues of accuracy. In *Activity 1*, students look at the advantages of simulations. As well as the safely aspect, students might think of cost advantages, the speed of obtaining results and the ability to repeat simulations with variations very easily.

*Activity 2* introduces a common scenario on many parts of the railway system; students simply load the file *Spreadsheet 2*. Students first need to understand how it works. The basic rule of rail safety, unchanged for years, is that the track is divided into sections and only one train is allowed in a section at a given time. Students are then exposed to more on/off, 1/2 computer basics.

Now revisit the IF function. *Activity 3* works through the use of the IF function where it is used to make decisions to control a signal.

*Activity 4* looks at conditional cell formatting, which is a powerful tool for setting up simulations. The colours of the signal are displayed in cells using this spreadsheet feature.

### Review
Address any difficulties here to clear up any problems that may still remain. Check that all the students are well aware of the importance of accuracy in setting up formulae and how spaces can lead to problems.

### Homework
Students should attempt to explain the formula using the type of representation given in the Student Book.

## Differentiation
Further uses of conditional cell formatting can be considered by more able students, perhaps in highlighting negative numbers in a household budget.

# What are websites? 30 31

## Curriculum link
**Framework coverage:** F1c
**SoW:** Unit 9
**NC:** 1b
**Prior learning:** The students will all have extensive experience of using the web.

## Resources
● Access to the Internet
● Worksheet 8

## Lesson guidance
This unit briefly revisits what the students know about web pages, but quickly moves on to the production of their own pages. The first lesson therefore covers much that will be already familiar to the students. However, look at the knowledge that they should possess in a more formal way, keeping in mind the understanding of ICT as a subject, usage of correct terminology and future tests. This unit includes rather more technical knowledge than previously.

### Starter
Using *Worksheet 8*, the students show some simple knowledge of web terminology.

### Development
The panel *The Internet* sets out some basic facts that students should know. There is the usual injunction to be wary about what you read because the source is not always totally clear. *Activity 1* involves one of several visits to the excellent *howstuffworks* website

for students to find out some fundamental things about the Internet.

The next panel takes a closer look at the nature of a website. The dynamic random nature of movement through a website is contrasted with the approach used to read a book. Bring the term 'hyperlink' to students' attention and its significance. In *Activity 2*, students focus their attention on how web pages can provide many advantages over printed material. They ought to recognise that, for looking up reference material, the ability to follow up promising leads can be a time saver. The information can also be more up to date if the site is well maintained. Also, the multimedia capabilities can be noted as an aid to immediacy and interest. Are there drawbacks too? Does surfing make us less patient?

The standard ways of navigation around a site and, indeed, the whole web, are the topic of the next panel. Remind students that browsers store all sorts of details about where they have been surfing and that this may have privacy implications. For *Activity 3*, students look at the good old standby for good web design, the BBC site, and are challenged to discover the hyperlinks.

The last panel addresses the issue of web page storage. The students need to understand that (a) data are distributed all over the world and (b) the pages are stored on servers. Compare the use of the word 'server' with the same term when applied to a LAN. In each case, it refers to a computer that provides files or services to others that are connected to it. For *Activity 4*, students investigate what server organisation holds the school website.

### Review
Internet terminology is reinforced by a 'make up questions for these answers' quiz.

### Homework
The homework tests knowledge of what has gone before. There is an opportunity for assessment here: better students will show a secure understanding of the main issues, with clear demarcation of the issues, whereas weaker students will only show a cursory grasp.

## Differentiation
More able students could be challenged to suggest how the computer 'knows' where the user has been in the correct reverse order when the back button is clicked. A few might suggest a data store of site addresses where a pointer is used to keep track of current position.

# Web tools 32 33

## Curriculum link
**Framework coverage:** E4b, E5b
**SoW:** Unit 9
**NC:** 3a
**Prior learning:** All the material in the preceding lesson plus plenty of Internet surfing experience

### Resources

- Word-processing software
- Access to the Internet
- Worksheet 9
- Worksheet 10
- CD: Image 1
- CD: Image 2

## Lesson guidance

In this lesson, basic software tools associated with the Internet are considered, first looking at viewing web pages, but concentrating most on appropriate software and file formats for posting material onto the web.

### Starter

The starter uses *Worksheet 9* to find a variety of Internet terms.

### Development

The panel *Why do we need browsers?* directs attention to the role of browser software in viewing web pages. For any students who still do not understand what the browser software actually does, take this opportunity to explain that web pages are not pages at all in any real sense, but consist of stored characters and associated program code. The characters contain a description of how the page is to be displayed. It is the job of the browser to turn these instructions into a visible page on the user's screen. Browsers are also able to interpret certain program instructions to make the web pages more exciting and interactive.

For *Activity 1*, students think of other things that a web browser can do. If the students are unsure of this, they will be able to find plenty of ideas by simply looking through the menus and toolbars that are part of their browser.

The panel called *Tools for making pages* is just the start of a look at how simple web pages can be constructed. There are so many ways of setting up pages these days – almost any generic software has a Save As Web Page or Save as HTML option. Users need to be a bit wary of making too much use of these features for reasons mentioned earlier. Sometimes, the HTML code produced can be extremely difficult to maintain.

It helps if students are first introduced to some simple HTML using a plain text editor; this is covered in the next lesson. For now, however, the full extent of the features available and the vast array of tools that exist for creating pages are briefly considered. In *Activity 2*, students visit a site where many tools and utilities are on offer. The students are simply expected to appreciate what a vast enterprise making web pages has become.

The students then look at the issue of uploading pages onto a web server. The details of this are beyond the scope of the present preview, but make students aware of the term 'FTP' and its significance. In *Activity 3*, students turn their attention to the large number of organisations that provide web hosting. The students will know of several of these already

from advertisements and if they consult with each other, a reasonably long list should be produced.

Students are next reminded about downloading issues and attention focused on file sizes and download times. This is much less of an issue than previously, as more and more people subscribe to broadband, but it is likely that file sizes will expand to fill the bandwidth available and infrastructure providers will constantly be playing 'catch-up'. *Activity 4* uses *Image 1* and *Image 2* to remind students how some file types (notably bitmaps) take much more storage space than compressed formats such as JPEGs. GIF files are also used a lot on websites. These are also compressed but often to a lesser extent that JPEGs. Animated GIFs display a succession of slightly different GIFs so they are likely to increase download times.

### Review

The class does its own review in this case and produces a summary of the general issues examined.

### Homework

*Worksheet 10* gives students a lead-in to the homework, where they are encouraged to compare the value for money of different providers. They may be reminded that this, just as with telephone and utility providers, is a constantly moving area and it is advantageous to check for value regularly.

## Differentiation

The lesson has been largely observational so the homework is the best opportunity to assess progress. More able students could look up the general principles about how images can be compressed. Methods of connecting to a broadband service could be researched and comparisons made of costs and benefits.

# Web page design features

34 35

## Curriculum link

**Framework coverage:** E1, E2
**SoW:** Unit 9
**NC:** 3a, 3b, 3c
**Prior learning:** None

## Resources

- Word-processing software
- Worksheet 11
- Worksheet 12
- CD: Website 1

## Lesson guidance

This lesson looks at some basic web page components and introduces some advice about conventions used when producing web pages. Appreciating these basic rules is important if later work is to be done efficiently. Stress to students that working in a methodical way will save them effort in the long run.

## Starter

The starter revisits Year 7 work and the issue of web page reliability. Revision like this can prove immensely valuable in making sure that all the concepts are remembered and reinforced. Indicators of reliability might centre on domain name suffixes. For example, some might have a degree of faith in a domain that ends with **.ac.uk**. It is worth considering whether the organisation that puts up the pages is recognisable or well known for trustworthiness. Otherwise, a degree of scepticism is reasonable.

## Development

The first panel names parts of a web page. Take time to highlight the terminology; it makes the development and communication of ideas so much easier. The panel examines a very basic web page and then, for *Activity 1*, students locate some of its basic features, the names of which they now know.

For *Activity 2*, students load up a sample website from the CD: *Website 1*. *Worksheet 11* is also needed. Students use this simple website to consolidate their knowledge about website components in a hands-on and interactive way.

Many students – and adults – build their own websites using various online tools. Often, the purpose of the website is not clear. The panel *Design is important* draws attention to a few basic ideas that should be borne in mind when designing a site. Emphasise that, at the very least, the designer ought to have a clear idea of the purpose of a website. In *Activity 3*, students then look at the overall structure of the demonstration site, and should work on their own to complete *Worksheet 12*.

How many times has it been next to impossible to find a student's work when the file name is effectively something random? Too often, students will choose file names that are inappropriate or that will have an adverse impact on their work's functionality. Emphasise that they need to be aware of naming conventions so as to make sure that the development process causes as few problems as possible. Cross-platform work is common when developing for the web. Most people develop using a PC in a *Windows* environment (a few might use Apples), but very many web servers are UNIX or Linux based and there are sometimes subtle differences that can cause gremlins if naming conventions are not followed. In *Activity 4*, students reflect on such problems. They may not have the necessary knowledge unless told, but they should be aware that, in their ordinary work, sensible file naming is an important part of what they do.

## Review

Discuss the main features of this lesson and encourage students to list these as bullet points.

## Homework

Recounting what they have learned by producing instructions for others to follow may help students to consolidate their knowledge. The guide to planning a website need only be brief, but it should assume no knowledge of the reader.

## Differentiation

The homework is the best opportunity for assessment here. Understanding of the basic ideas and being able to express them clearly will provide suitable differentiation.

# An introduction to HTML

36 37

## Curriculum link

**Framework coverage:** E6, E7
**SoW:** Unit 9
**NC:** 3c
**Prior learning:** Previous work on the Internet

## Resources

- Text editor such as Microsoft *NotePad*
- Access to the Internet
- Worksheet 13

## Lesson guidance

In this lesson, students learn about the basic structure of HTML. Maintaining web pages is greatly assisted by some knowledge of HTML; small adjustments can be made which might be difficult with authoring software. Apart from giving a greater understanding of how web pages work, if students look at the HTML it will help them to develop a general comprehension of computer issues, such as word-processing file formats and programming.

## Starter

*Worksheet 13* is required for this activity, which has to be carried out in pairs. Students should learn that providing an accurate description of a page requires care and a little specialist vocabulary. They should also gain an insight to some issues concerned with page layout and formatting.

## Development

The *What is HTML?* panel looks at some basic background information. Essentially, there are codes or tags embedded in the text of a web page, which tell the browser how to display the text of the page. This is nothing new; embedded codes have long been a feature of word-processed documents, and are used to allow the display of special effects that are now commonplace in documents, such as bold and italic. In *Activity 1*, students discover the history of the development of the web. This is well worth doing, not only for its basic educational importance, but also because it helps students' understanding of where the web fits into the general progress and history of IT and communications.

The panel *A simple web page* shows the relationship between tags and the displayed page. Check that students appreciate how each line is set up. They should also realise that it is possible to set up a web page by simply typing in the text with the appropriate tags. Emphasise how useful it can be to be able to adjust the native HTML code when fine-tuning a website. For *Activity 2*, students access any web page to look at some HTML source 'code'. The amount visible may vary a lot depending on how the page was set up but, at the very least, the students should recognise roughly what is going on. If a complex page only shows up a little HTML, explain to students that it makes connections with other files that are not visible. Students can work on their own or in pairs on this activity. They may like to paste some of the code into a word processor and to make a few comments in another font or colour to indicate what they recognise.

The *Some more tags* panel looks at common formatting techniques. Check, through *Activity 3*, that students realise that HTML code, like many forms of computer encoding, is quite understandable. They should have little difficulty in recognising the alignment codes; most should also identify the bold and the italic tags.

For *Activity 4*, students write a simple page of their own. Allow time for this, especially because students might make little technical errors. Use a plain text editor such as *NotePad* because, although *Word* or *WordPad* will do the job, the alternatives offer more scope for confusion when having to save the work as a plain text file. (If this is not done, other control codes are saved alongside the HTML code and, as a result, the page will not work.) Stress what a text editor can do and why it is preferable to a word processor when writing any sort of code. The students are asked to open their saved file by double clicking. This can be done either in Windows *Explorer* or via *My Computer* and should load their work into the web browser. The students might notice that, in some file views, their work will now show up with a web page icon because they put in the .htm extension.

### Review
Lots of different skills are used through this lesson. Highlight some of the problems that arose while developing the web pages; students can gain much by listening to how other people solve problems.

### Homework
For this recap on what has gone before, the emphasis should be on clarity and brevity. A set of bullet point instructions without the need for much commentary should be sufficient.

## Differentiation
As an interesting extension, suggest that students type a very brief piece of text using their word processors. Make some of the text bold and some italic. Save the work as a *Word* file and another copy in rich text format (RTF). If the files are re-opened using a plain text editor such as *NotePad*, the use of embedded characters in documents becomes apparent. The RTF version will illustrate the point better. Students should see that the basic approach is not too different to HTML.

There is an opportunity for assessment here by looking at which students are able to make the connections between HTML and RTF.

# Some more HTML

## Curriculum link
**Framework coverage:** E7
**SoW:** Unit 9
**NC:** 3c
**Prior learning:** Previous work on HTML

## Resources
- Text editor software
- Access to the Internet
- Worksheet 14
- Worksheet 15

## Lesson guidance
This lesson looks at basic HTML instructions to add colours and some interactivity using hyperlinks. These features can be implemented in any HTML editor, but there is much value in continuing to see exactly what is happening by using a basic text editor.

### Starter
This quick revision activity, intended for individual completion, requires *Worksheet 14*.

### Development
The first section is concerned with a way of editing a web page. Most web browser toolbars have a button that, when pressed, opens the HTML of the web page being looked at into a suitable editor. The system may be set up to use *WordPad* or *NotePad* or, maybe, *Word*. *Activity 1* requires the students to load the page worked on in the last lesson into the browser and then to select the edit function. Remind students that the changed version must be saved and then they must click the Refresh button in the browser.

The next panel, *Using colours*, shows some simple tags for coding basic colours. To handle a wide range of colours, code numbers are given. Most students, at this stage, will just have to accept that these codes are given in hexadecimal; more able students could easily cope with a brief extension to explain hexadecimal numbers. As long as some notion of codes for numbers is absorbed, the students will be doing well. A little practice in editing colours is provided in *Activity 2*.

The whole attraction of the Internet is in the ability to move from place to place by means of a click, i.e. using hyperlinks. The Student Book shows how tags are set up to make hyperlinks. For *Activity 3*, students set up a hyperlink by adding it manually to the HTML code. This is best done by using the edit method described in *Activity 1*. Remind students to save and refresh again. This would work well in paired or individual activity.

The students have been working with a single page up to this point. In *Activity 4*, they make an extra page. Tell them that a real website is made up of lots of pages but there can't be any useful internal links until the extra pages are created. *Worksheet 15* provides the instructions for this activity. As ever, stress the importance of using suitable file names with the right extension.

### Review
In the summing up, recall briefly the extra features, but encourage students to think about features they have seen on real websites and to comment on how they could enhance what they have done so far.

### Homework
This homework revision exercise can be used for continuing assessment. When the homework is completed, consider comparing the words and definitions produced by different class members.

## Differentiation
One interesting extension activity would be to look into hexadecimal numbers more closely. More able students could work out what the numbers given in the text mean in decimal notation.

# Using Microsoft *Word* to make a web page

40 41

## Curriculum link
**Framework coverage:** D1b, E6, E7
**SoW:** Unit 9
**NC:** 3b, 3c
**Prior learning:** Previous experience of word processing

## Resources
• Word-processor software, such as Microsoft *Word,* with 'save as HTML' capability

## Lesson guidance
The students have now made simple web pages using a text editor, but to make more elaborate pages requires more sophisticated tools, such as a dedicated web page editor. Most generic software is capable of producing HTML code, thereby saving a lot of time. Microsoft *Word* can be used as a web editor; however, it does produce lots of unnecessary HTML code which can then make it difficult to edit. Nevertheless, sometimes *Word* is useful to produce something quickly or to convert an existing document into web form. The pros and cons of this approach are for the students to consider in the activities.

### Starter
Students consider all the things that they find useful about their word processor. Ensure that they mention text formatting, picture and table insertion, shortcuts and the like. The group list should make it clear that many people depend on word-processor tools to be productive. This contrasts with the limited capabilities of a text editor and the hard work that goes into producing a web page.

### Development
A document can be saved in HTML format by most modern word processors. Students will learn how to do this as instructed in *Activity 1*. Point out that, at the same time, there are several other file formats available, such as RTF, which some students may have used in an earlier lesson.

Many people who use word processors do not make full use of the best time-savers, such as the style feature. There are so many advantages in using this when making standard type faces for headings and sub-headings that it should be a matter of routine. The Student Book draws attention to the style box. Tell students the shortcuts for the three levels of headings – ctrl-alt-1 or ctrl-alt-2 or ctrl-alt-3 – and encourage them to use them. These headings can translate directly to the HTML top-level headings.

Many web pages are enhanced by having a coloured background. For *Activity 2*, students find out how to change the background colour using *Word* (Format – Background) and then how to make a page with this colour. Encourage those who need further consolidation to search through the help screens available by pressing F1. Tell students that help screens offer another example of the use of hypertext. Instruct students, when they save this new page, to give it a different name from their last page so that they have them both for the next exercise.

Students are now asked to compare how easy it was to produce a page using *Word* with the same process using a text editor. They will probably realise that it is a lot easier to use a word processor and that more features are available. *Activity 3* brings home to them how some software produces really messy HTML. Often that doesn't matter and the advantages make it all worthwhile. In *Activity 4*, students consider whether there are any advantages to be gained from adding all this extra code. Mostly, the answer is that there are very few advantages – it is put there 'just in case it's needed'. Browsers can make a good job of displaying pages without needing to be told this amount of detail.

### Review
Give further consideration to using *Word* and the file sizes of the two seemingly identical web pages. Students can use *My Computer* or *Windows Explorer* to do this. (The *Word* version is bigger.)

### Homework
Students are now given some freedom to let their imagination roam. If there is time, students may like to put their designs into practice. This then provides an opportunity for assessment, with regard to their integrating material for a bigger purpose.

## Differentiation
Able students who are working quickly could experiment by taking the HTML code from a *Word* generated page and trying to eliminate some of the code without making any difference to the final product.

# Using *FrontPage*

42 43

## Curriculum link

**Framework coverage:** E2
**SoW:** Unit 9
**NC:** 3b, 3c
**Prior learning:** None

## Resources

- Web-authoring tools, e.g. *FrontPage*
- Worksheet 16
- CD: Website 1

## Lesson guidance

*Word* is rarely used to create serious web pages. Coding it all in HTML is fine if you have the know-how and the time. However, most people will choose one of the many web-authoring packages designed for the job, such as *FrontPage* or *Dreamweaver*. This book focuses on Microsoft *FrontPage*; this is no comment on its pros and cons, but simply because it is widely available in schools and it has many useful web maintenance features that are also easy to use. The HTML code it produces is generally quite 'clean'. If your school has a different authoring package such as *Dreamweaver*, the exercises and comments can still be used, although the actual commands and screens will vary somewhat.

### Starter

*Worksheet 16* is required for the starter. Students work individually to fit the words into the grid.

### Development

The *What is FrontPage?* panel introduces the software and highlights one of its more attractive features i.e. that it is a WYSIWYG package. Point out to students that, although there is a wide choice of software to do any particular task, choosing the right tool for the job can make life a lot easier.

In *Activity 1* students need access to the CD files in *Website 1*, so you need to copy this folder to a suitable location. On a network, this may be a specially created directory in the student's own user directory. Avoid mixing these with all the other work of a student; confusion will result and this may lead to things not working later. The website is then loaded into *FrontPage* using the *Open Web* option.

The *Different views* panel points out how a good web-authoring package not only lets you write HTML code without having to know the details, but also provides management tools that help you to view and update the entire site. In *Activity 2*, students familiarise themselves with some of the views available in the authoring package.

The *Rules for a good website* panel offers straightforward advice for making an effective site. Students may need a lot of time for *Activity 3* – as individuals or pairs – to put into practice some of the ideas that they have been given and also to add to the basic rules.

The *Using tables* panel stresses how important tables are, so reinforce this message to the *n*th degree! Students need to understand that they cannot drag and drop images and text wherever they want on a web page. The inherent simplicity of HTML, even today, restricts what you can do with layout. As the Student Book says, the way to handle layout is with tables. Tables can be used to form grids of any size so that elements can be dropped in more or less where they are wanted. You can even have tables inside the cells of other tables, so once the principle is firmly grasped, the restrictions are not that great! Tables can be created in a fully WYSIWYG way with *FrontPage* and other web editors, so the HTML code needn't be learned (although it is interesting and sometimes useful to look at it). For *Activity 4*, students produce tables and see what can be done with them; however, restrict this to text at the moment.

### Review

All the foregoing issues can be brought together in the review and different views can be considered. After all, the choice of software is not a hard and fast business – everyone will have preferences and prejudices!

### Homework

The unit is heading towards producing a website for the year group. The homework is preparation for this by asking around for ideas. A good student will categorise the ideas and present them clearly and logically.

## Differentiation

More able students can gain much by looking carefully at the HTML produced by *FrontPage*. They could produce a brief report on how it compares with *Word*-produced code and how much 'unnecessary' material there seems to be in it. For a simple page, there won't be much clutter.

# A school website

44 45

## Curriculum link

**Framework coverage:** E1, E4a
**SoW:** Unit 9
**NC:** 3a, 3b
**Prior learning:** Previous lessons in this unit

## Resources

- Web-authoring tools
- Access to the Internet

## Lesson guidance

The next five lessons move further towards integrated projects, and this approach continues in other units in Year 8, into Year 9 and beyond. Students need to bring together a range of experiences to create a useful and well-executed final product: a website specific to Year 8 issues.

These lessons are devoted to this theme and provide an ideal opportunity for group working. This is a good idea for all sorts of reasons, not least because working in teams is what happens in real-life systems development.

## Starter

The first step is to generate ideas that could be useful in a Year 8 website. At this stage, these ideas need not be too focused, so encourage a free-ranging discussion. This may result in ideas that you might not anticipate but would appeal to the students and hence be useful to the site.

## Development

The main parts that will be required for the website need to be identified. In *Activity 1,* groups are formed, so that each group can devote itself to the production of pages on a particular topic. You may need to intervene to make sure that the workload is spread sensibly and that achievable component parts are determined.

The basic design points of the website are considered next. For *Activity 2,* students consider how other websites have been laid out to catch the attention of passing surfers. The students can suggest their own ideas about what grabs attention. It may be a clear easy-to-use interface or, possibly, a moving image. They will also need to think about which ideas are achievable in the available time.

In *Activity 3,* students – in their chosen groups – decide what information is to be presented on the website. The mind map provided in the Student Book might help to focus their minds on the principal categories of information. However, encourage students to deviate from this if they have better ideas of their own. Check that, for each group, the work is fairly allocated within the group. Recommend that ideas are separately typed up by the groups, and then made available in a common area of the network, so that a 'global' plan is accessible to all.

Next, some consideration is given to the physical structure of the pages and especially to the use of hover buttons. These are common on websites, so encourage students to include them. In *Activity 4,* students have time to explore how to produce hover buttons in *FrontPage* (or whatever other software is being used).

## Review

Establish the final allocation of work so that everyone knows exactly what to do and how each group's work fits together to create the entire website. Make this plan available so that they can all make reference to it when necessary.

## Homework

Individuals make a draft of their own textual contributions for homework. This does not need to be well formed at this stage, as editing will undoubtedly take place later.

## Differentiation

The most useful way to add extra opportunities here would be to explore the page-authoring software to find out other special effects that might be implemented on the website, e.g. the use of frames.

# Mapping out the site

## Curriculum link

**Framework coverage:** E6, E7
**SoW:** Unit 9
**NC:** 3a, 3b
**Prior learning:** Previous lessons in this unit, coupled with practical experience of organising files and directories will be helpful.

## Resources

● Worksheet 17

## Suggested web addresses

● **www.ed-phys.fr/htbin/ipaddress**
● **www.howstuffworks.com**

## Lesson guidance

Websites can become fiendishly complex after a very short time, with many component parts and resources dependent on each other. A well-organised site is much less likely to contain irritating anomalies such as broken links and non-existent images. So, this lesson is concerned with keeping the website organised. Emphasise the importance of this to students, and stress that good organisation will save them effort in the long run.

## Starter

Using *Worksheet 17,* students work on their own, each completing the planning of the site, starting from the basics of a simple idea for a personal website, and supplying the missing page diagrams and arrows.

## Development

The need to keep the site co-ordinated is raised first. The site is to be constructed by several groups, so to keep the links working requires some planning. It would be helpful to have prior knowledge of file names so that this can be done. In *Activity 1,* responsibilities are arranged.

The *Map the site* panel shows how part of a site map can look. Initially, not all the links will be shown. It requires some care to put this on paper in such a way that the links remain clear, so some over-simplification may be necessary at this stage. In *Activity 2,* each group plans, exclusively, their part of the site in this way. Later, the parts can be put together.

The *What's in a name?* panel takes a break from planning to look at domain names, and explains that web addresses are stored as numbers called IP (Internet protocol) addresses. You could add that they are in the form of 4 numbers (octets), each one having a maximum value of 255, such as 65.214.36.146. Several websites, such as **www.ed-phys.fr/htbin/ipaddress**, will reveal your own current web address, but this is covered in the next lesson. The difficulty people have in remembering numbers explains why domain names are used instead. In *Activity 3,* students look at the issue of managing domain names.

For *Activity 4*, students plan the folders where they will store their website resources. Stress that meaningful folder names need to be devised.

### Review
The review exercise makes further use of that versatile resource, the BBC site, and asks for some practical suggestions about how the pages might be stored.

### Homework
The file organisation theme is reinforced with this homework but the focus is a little wider so that the student is asked to consider local disk organisation for general file management. Assessment can be built into this exercise because it is on an individual basis and checks how well the concepts have been understood.

## Differentiation
Extension work can be done in further looking up how domain name servers work. howstuffworks.com is a good source as usual.

# Building better pages  48 | 49
## Curriculum link
**Framework coverage:** E5a
**SoW:** Unit 9
**NC:** 3b, 3c
**Prior learning:** Previous lessons in this unit

## Resources
● Access to the Internet

## Lesson guidance
This lesson explores general website issues, with a diversion to look at IP addresses.

### Starter
The starter expects the students to identify the idea of a house style. To make this concept more familiar, suggest they think about how any company promotes itself. The students, as a whole class activity, should then suggest ideas such as colour schemes, fonts used and many other *look* and *feel* matters.

### Development
The first panel asks the students to briefly reflect on how satisfied they are with the results of their previous planning activities. They then quickly move on to *Activity 1* and decide on file names; these will probably be different from the page name as displayed in the browser. The page name is for public consumption, but the file name is for the students' own organisational convenience.

IP addresses are considered again and, in *Activity 2*, students visit another website to look up their IP address. Even if this was touched on in the previous lesson, check that students know the term IP address, have a basic understanding of what it means and understand why name equivalents are used.

The next panel continues the styling questions. Websites that have a consistent look give a much better impression of trustworthiness and, for *Activity 3*, students need to think through the issue of consistency.

Images are often a difficult problem when building sites. So often, students' work looks OK on one occasion, but later, images disappear. This happens particularly when they work on their material at home and then bring it in. Stress to students that pasting images into place is not the way to include an image on a web page. Separate image files are needed; and these need to be stored in a separate and dedicated images folder.

Apart from the technicalities of image use, there are also issues of safety. In *Activity 4*, the danger of students posting images of themselves on a public website are raised. More able students will read this for themselves; for some groups, it may be best if you read this and make a few summary points about the care that needs to be taken.

### Review
The Year 8 theme is set aside while general ideas about content are considered.

### Homework
For this homework, images are to be collected. These may be pictures to scan or digital images from cameras. Students who have difficulty in arranging this should be encouraged to bring ideas for images, which can be generated in class.

## Differentiation
Students could look further at safety issues and list rules that they could recommend to avoid any sort of harm while using the Internet. The importance of anonymity could be explored. The safety issues could go beyond personal safety and consider financial security as well. Consideration of wider issues is a suitable discriminator to allow assessment at higher levels.

# Developing the site  50 | 51
## Curriculum link
**Framework coverage:** E5b, E7
**SoW:** Unit 9
**NC:** 3c, 4a
**Prior learning:** Previous lessons in this unit; editing HTML

## Resources
● Web-authoring software or text editor

## Lesson guidance
This lesson focuses on the many issues about website development and maintenance accessible to Year 8 students. With their extensive surfing experience, they should have opinions on many of these issues.

## Starter

Use a brief discussion with the class to lead in to what follows. Many websites are less effective than they might be because they are out of date. With some sites, this does not matter. Give consideration to what sort of sites need updating all the time, which ones need fairly regular maintenance and which can be left for a long time without losing their usefulness.

## Development

Broken links are always frustrating and they give a very poor impression of whoever put up the site. Ask students to think of any occasions when this has been particularly annoying. In *Activity 1*, students make a checklist of their own links as a means of keeping them up to date. This list can be produced by each group and combined later as a class resource if further development is anticipated.

As usual, a little extra effort can make life easier later on. The helpfulness of date and time stamping is brought out next and, in *Activity 2*, students add this information. This can be done very easily with a text editor, but if web-authoring software is used, students will see that it does not affect the display.

The Student Book then considers various methods of physically bringing the students' work together. Floppy disks seem to be increasingly unreliable these days, so using networked facilities is more likely to work well. You may like to consider the use of inexpensive 'memory sticks' that plug into the USB ports and store lots of data very rapidly. (Buy them online for the cheapest ones!) *Activity 3* deals with this.

*Activity 4* focuses attention on copyright. Stress that copying material that someone else has made raises moral and legal issues. When people work on a resource, it is only right that they should have their efforts acknowledged. It is annoying to have one's ideas used by others who claim them as their own. Some material is clearly in the public domain and the authors intend it to be so, but the students should be clear about what is and is not reasonable.

## Review

Have a class discussion on updating sites; this can range into reasons why other sites need to be updated. (See differentiation section.)

## Homework

Asking for the views of others is a useful discipline when creating anything for public consumption. It is a good idea to bring in someone else as well as peers and teachers. The student should write up the comments for assessment purposes.

## Differentiation

Students who are working quickly can visit a number of sites and write comments on how often they need to be updated to retain their usefulness. This activity could provide assessment opportunities to distinguish higher-level students.

# Testing and evaluating the site

## Curriculum link

**Framework coverage:** D7b
**SoW:** Unit 9
**NC:** 3a, 3c
**Prior learning:** Previous lessons in this unit

## Resources

- Word-processing software
- Access to the Internet

## Suggested web addresses

- **www.howstuffworks.com/**

## Lesson guidance

This lesson is a final look at how well the website turned out. It also takes the opportunity to look at a few other web issues that have relevance to evaluation.

## Starter

The starter looks briefly at the opinions of others as gathered in the previous homework. A global list of comments can be made available on screen or the whiteboard for the whole class to consider.

## Development

The purposes of the site are itemised. In *Activity 1*, students ask themselves, honestly, how well they have fulfilled the project brief. They can do this in groups and, later, compare what they think with others.

Cookies are the topic of the next panel. Initiate a brief discussion about the good and bad points about using cookies. Stress that cookies are just small text files of information; they are *not* programs and they cannot actually *do* anything. For *Activity 2*, students access a source of information about cookies.

Guest books are common on websites. In *Activity 3*, students consider whether a guest book is a good idea. The answer to this will vary according to the site; students may want to focus on their own website and consider the usefulness of having a guest book. They could also consider to what degree a guest book should be 'moderated' by the site owner.

In groups, or in pairs, the completed site can be looked at. The evaluation report prepared for *Activity 4* will be much easier if the students use the bullet points in the Student Book as sub headings.

## Review

The evaluations are presented to the class with the good and bad points separated. It might be useful for later assessment purposes if each individual makes a summary at some point, although this should be kept brief.

### Homework

Many websites seek opinions from their readers. In the homework, students design a suitable web form to collect information that may be of use. They should make sure that the form actually looks like a web form with suitable objects to collect the required information, such as drop-down boxes and text boxes, cancel and submit buttons.

### Differentiation

Cookies are well worth looking into. As well as the link given in the Student Book, as usual howstuffworks is worth a visit. More able students can look here to find out more about cookies and perhaps produce a summary of why people sometimes worry about cookies and how much they need to. As usual, a more in-depth and thoughtful approach could be a good opportunity for assessing at higher levels.

## Who holds data on me?

`54 | 55`

### Curriculum link

**Framework coverage:** F7b, F7c
**SoW:** Unit 10
**NC:** 3a, 4b, 5d
**Prior learning:** Year 7 work on databases (F9a, F9b: Book 1 pp. 76–81)

### Resources

- Word-processing software
- Worksheet 18

### Lesson guidance

The first two lessons in this unit consider data and look at it in various scenarios, but visit other ICT concerns along the way. Many practical skills are covered in some detail, as well as theory knowledge.

### Starter

Students should know how databases make searching for data easier and more secure as well as allowing the combining of data from various sources. They should also be aware that databases and their manipulation form the heart of most businesses these days and constitute by far the most common reason for computer use by organisations. This starter gives an opportunity to revise these aspects of databases.

### Development

Starting locally, students consider the data that are certainly held on them on the school's computer system. For *Activity 1*, students think about why this data might be held. *Activity 2* requires students to identify details that they think might be useful to the school. A check with your school's admin staff could show that as many as 60 fields are maintained about each student.

The *Personal data* panel leads to the topic of the Data Protection Act (covered in the next lesson) and

problems concerned with privacy. *Activity 3* spreads the thinking wider to bring about the realisation that 'out there' enormous amounts of data are stored about people.

*Activity 4* counters any concerns by considering the many good reasons for storing personal data and how the school is helped to function by keeping this level of detail about each student.

In many circumstances, there are opportunities to collect data, and these data are a very valuable commodity. In *Activity 5*, students consider one such scenario: booking a holiday. They might suggest organisations such as the travel agent, the insurance company, hotels, airlines and the tour organiser.

### Review

Highlight the vast amount of data collected and emphasise that it can help to make our lives more comfortable, as well as posing some concerns.

### Homework

Students use *Worksheet 18* to look at the consequences of personal data being held. Communicating with individuals is much enhanced although not always to our liking.

### Differentiation

There is no need to go much beyond the outline as yet. Extension work could centre on some of the less obvious fields in the student database such as mode of transport to school or whether packed lunches are brought. Students could be asked to comment on why these fields might be needed.

## The Data Protection Act

`56 | 57`

### Curriculum link

**Framework coverage:** F7c
**SoW:** Unit 10
**NC:** 4b
**Prior learning:** Year 7 work (F2: Book 1 p. 79)

### Resources

- Access to the Internet
- Worksheet 19

### Lesson guidance

During this lesson, students learn why data protection legislation is thought necessary and how most countries have similar laws.

### Starter

Students should begin to realise how much detail can be obtained about people's movements. Mobile phone records can pinpoint people's locations with great accuracy while their phones are switched on. This is particularly true in cities where the base stations are much closer together than in rural areas.

Movements can also be logged to a degree by making use of credit card transactions, traffic cameras and, in particular, the congestion charge system in London (although it discards each day's records for those who have paid the charge).

### Development

In *Activity 1*, students complete a simple web-based exercise to look up the role of the government office that deals with data protection. The role of the Information Commissioner is then made a little more immediate. For *Activity 2*, students visit another website to find out the nature of the data allowable in the school under the Act. Stress that much of the information held has come from their parents; some is administrative and has come from the head and other staff of the school.

The provisions of the Data Protection Act are now looked at. In *Activity 3*, students speculate on some reasons why infringements of the Act are of real concern to people. Clearly, in this case, the data are not being held securely, are not accurate and there are worries that unauthorised people might gain access to details such as the cleaner's address.

For *Activity 4*, students demonstrate how quickly data can be sent from one place to another, thereby making hacking and other nefarious usage of data much easier. Also, even with the legitimate usage of data, transferring it around is so fast and easy that there are concerns about how all this intelligence on individuals might be used. In *Activity 5*, students list reasons why there are legitimate concerns about so much data being available. Their reasons could include the encouragement of mail shots, spam and other direct marketing, excessive national and local government interference and easier probing of one's affairs by police and Inland Revenue authorities.

### Review

While looking over the main matters covered in this lesson, students list some practical steps that the school can take to comply with the DPA. Such measures will include not leaving logged-on computers unattended, remembering to change passwords regularly and sending copies of the data to parents on a regular basis for verification.

### Homework

Students complete *Worksheet 19* to show why their school needs to hold data about them. Then, in preparation for the next lesson, the students recall what they have to do when logging on to their network, plus the steps they need to take when performing other network tasks.

## Differentiation

Differentiation will be clear during the activities in this lesson. The number of different concerns and measures identified by students will provide an opportunity for assessment. Extension work could involve exploring the Internet for details of the data protection legislation in different countries.

# Networks

## Curriculum link

**Framework coverage:** F7a, F7b
**SoW:** Unit 10
**NC:** 1a, 1b
**Prior learning:** Experience of using networks; network coverage in Year 7

## Resources

- Word-processing software
- Worksheet 20
- Worksheet 21
- Availability of technical staff (or whoever looks after the network)

## Lesson guidance

Nowadays, most organisations use computer networks, having abandoned their old mainframe systems, to take advantage of the cost-effectiveness and flexibility that networks bring. Most schools also have networks so it is important that the students understand what is going on. Such understanding will help them to use the resources more effectively; it also provides reasons for some of the rules that they have to follow for network safety.

The pace of this lesson should be fairly rapid to cover as much as possible, and not all students will complete everything. However, this can be used to help in assessment.

### Starter

Understanding networks starts with a consideration of the steps that students follow to log on and start working on the school network. When they have made lists of their understanding of the process, bring them together to consider their answers and to check them for accuracy.

### Development

The word 'peripheral' is used here and students should ensure that they note it, possibly by adding it to their glossary. In *Activity 1*, students look at the range of peripherals available to them. Some might not be connected and some teacher help may be required.

Explain the role of the server and the fact that some networks have many servers (e.g. printer server, mail server). Mention also the idea of a client machine and encourage students to add these new terms to their glossaries. For *Activity 2*, students need to research the school's network; you may prefer to have the information to hand and to supply it *after* the students have speculated on what is present.

Most of the advantages of using networks are concerned with sharing resources. For *Activity 3*, students use *Worksheet 20* to focus their thinking on *what* is shared in the school network, and by whom.

Some common network problems are then considered. In *Activity 4*, students use *Worksheet 21* to find out how such problems are dealt with in the school. It might be helpful if any technical staff are available to answer their questions.

### Review

Many advantages of networks have been discussed. Students produce a final list of some of the main reasons for having a network in the school as a group exercise. Make this global list available to the students for revision purposes.

### Homework

Individuals show their general knowledge about automatic data input in preparation for the next lesson.

## Differentiation

The sharing of data is one of the most important reasons for having a network. Students who are working quickly could make a list of data that needs to be shared on a school network, and identify those who need to have access to some of the shared data.

# Automatic data collection

`60` `61`

## Curriculum link

**Framework coverage:** F7a
**SoW:** Unit 10
**NC:** 4b, 5d
**Prior learning:** Previous work on databases

## Resources

- Access to the Internet
- Worksheet 22

## Lesson guidance

This lesson looks at ways in which data are input into a computer system automatically. Students need to be aware that manually entering data into a computer is time-consuming and error prone. Consequently, any method of automating the process is likely to be of value to a business. Much of this lesson is, of necessity, instructional. Samples of the methods mentioned would help to improve delivery.

### Starter

Students will be familiar with bar codes, having seen them on groceries and other goods. For this starter activity, the class brainstorms all the different places where bar codes are used such as books, parcels in transit, new cars in transit, warehouse systems and car parks.

### Development

Stress the difference between data and information. The rationale behind automated data entry is first discussed with the group and the common methods of doing this are listed but not talked about in depth yet. In *Activity 1*, students are given a deliberately vague form to fill in on *Worksheet 22*, to gather information that they will all know about. Use this activity to show how care must be taken when organising any data capture to make sure that the intended data are indeed captured.

For the *Bar codes* panel, stress that bar codes do not hold a lot of data and are only a means of identifying an item. For example, the price of a good such as a can of beans is not encoded within its bar code. Many websites put up by bar code software companies demonstrate the production of a bar code from an identification number. For *Activity 2*, students visit such a site.

OMR forms, covered next, should be familiar to students from a variety of contexts. In completing *Activity 3*, students might suggest entering lottery numbers, taking a class register, ordering goods from a form and/or collecting exam marks from marked papers.

OCR is used in turn-around documents such as gas meter readings, but it is more likely to be familiar as a means of turning a scanned document into a word-processed file. For *Activity 4*, students might suggest editing old documents where there is no access to a computer-saved copy, or any other situation where the original file is not available such as old exam questions.

Finally, bring other common methods of automated data capture to the attention of the students: MICR, magnetic strips and smart cards. For *Activity 5*, students list further uses of card-based data. Their examples could include cash cards (not common in the UK), identity cards, phone cards, digital viewing cards and SIM cards in phones.

### Review

Encourage students to think of other ways of capturing data automatically. There are plenty of examples from their data logging experiences as well as the mobile phone logging mentioned earlier.

### Homework

Plenty of examples of electronic equipment with which students are familiar have data input; microwaves, videos, televisions, DVD players and cameras are obvious examples. Digital viewing boxes receive data automatically from the provider.

## Differentiation

The homework will provide a lot of discriminators for assessment. Extension activities could look at actions or facilities that would not be available if it were not for automatic data capture, such as bank machines and mobile phones.

# EPOS and EFTPOS

`62` `63`

## Curriculum link

**Framework coverage:** F7a, F7b
**SoW:** Unit 10
**NC:** 4b, 5d
**Prior learning:** Previous lessons in this unit

## Resources

- Access to the Internet
- Worksheet 23

## Lesson guidance

Many aspects of supermarket computer use are covered in this lesson. The students will mostly be working in pairs but you need to bring the class together frequently to make sure that they have the correct information. Aim to maintain a quick pace through the material.

### Starter

Some students will understand computer systems enough to suggest that the prices are stored on a database, and that the database is made available online to the checkouts. Some will realise that some form of network is necessary for this operation.

### Development

Introduce the term EPOS. In *Activity 1*, students should recognise that, even with a generally effective computer system, things do not always go according to plan. The problems that can slow down progress include anything from system failure, to bar codes that won't scan, credit cards that are rejected, too many money-off coupons to process, the necessity to do some things manually and many problems that are the result of human behaviour rather than IT glitches.

The link between bar codes and the ISBN of a book is examined and, for *Activity 2*, students look up the details of books that they may have available. They can also use this site to compare prices of books.

Comment on how computer systems linked to EPOS systems are useful for supermarket stock control. In *Activity 3*, students list information needed to allow a stock control system to work, such as the number in stock, reorder level, reorder quantity and date last ordered.

The benefits of EPOS to the shopper are itemised in the Student Book and, in *Activity 4*, students work in pairs or as individuals to think of reasons why automatic stock control might go wrong. Reasons could include theft, damage or incorrect figures entered when deliveries occur.

The distinction between EPOS and EFTPOS can now be made, mentioning the benefits of paying by card that such systems bring. Disadvantages of EFTPOS are few, but for *Activity 5*, students might suggest overspending and system failure that can lead to not being able to do the shopping.

For *Activity 6*, students focus on the hardware needed for an EFTPOS system and use *Worksheet 23* to help them to list this quickly.

### Review

Briefly summarise the points raised, giving emphasis to clear thinking about who benefits from and who is disadvantaged by EFTPOS systems. In many cases, both shopper and shop benefit, but for different reasons.

### Homework

The homework checks understanding by looking at another networked system. Students should be able to identify keypads and card readers as input devices, and screen, money dispenser and receipt printer as output. They may be able to deduce that a network card or connection plus telephone link could also be involved. The next session is also preempted.

## Differentiation

This will generally be by outcome. There is a lot to cover and not all the students will manage to produce all the answers suggested.

# Loyalty cards

64 65

## Curriculum link

**Framework coverage:** F7a
**SoW:** Unit 10
**NC:** 4a, 4b, 5d
**Prior learning:** Basic database knowledge

## Resources

- Word processor
- Access to the Internet
- Worksheet 24

## Lesson guidance

This lesson looks at the familiar loyalty cards that are used by many large retailers and would never have existed in such quantity without the information systems that back them up. In the past, shoppers sometimes collected stamps when they made their purchases; IT solutions have brought much more power to retailers who are taking advantage of the value of the extra information available to them.

### Starter

For this easy starter, get students to think of businesses that issue loyalty cards. It should not take them long to produce a fairly long list as this recaps their homework from the previous lesson.

### Development

The *How do loyalty cards work?* panel gives a quick introduction to the basic idea of a loyalty card system. In *Activity 1*, students list ways in which the bonuses from point accumulation are issued to customers, e.g. as special offers, money-off coupons, air miles or reductions for other purchases.

The Student Book then looks at how customers apply for loyalty cards. In *Activity 2*, using *Worksheet 24*, which shows the sort of questions that are asked before a loyalty card is issued, students consider why all this information is needed. Some students may realise that direct marketing can be targeted more effectively if lots of details are known about an individual.

In *Activity 3*, students look at card-sharing by businesses. The added advantages that students might identify could be more information gathered in one place about the shopper's profile, thus giving more opportunities for direct marketing. The shopper is supposed to be able to accumulate points more quickly when they are available in lots of outlets. In fact, there is discontent that such schemes may be less generous than single company cards. The references in *Follow the mouse* look at these issues.

For *Activity 4,* students look at one example of how marketing can be more accurately focused. Students should recognise that the customers' shopping habits have been recorded and that database software can easily pick out customers who have not used a particular department in the store. The success can be judged by counting the number of returned coupons.

### Review

Use this review as a revision aid to ensure that the distinction is made between the beneficiaries of such schemes.

### Homework

For homework, students think about why there might be problems for the supermarket in running these schemes. There is always a chance that they are simply not cost-effective. Also there is the problem of what to do with the data. There are storage and processing concerns that might make the management wonder if it is worth all the time and investment.

A till receipt is needed for the next lesson, so ask students to each bring one.

### Differentiation

Students could spend more time on *Activity 4* and speculate about what fields would need to be incorporated into the databases to make this search possible.

# Supermarket till receipts

66 | 67

## Curriculum link

**Framework coverage:** F6a, F7a
**SoW:** Unit 10
**NC:** 1c, 3b
**Prior learning:** Database knowledge from Year 7 (F9a, F9b: Book 1 p. 84)

## Resources

- Database management software, such as *Access*
- Worksheet 25
- Worksheet 26
- Spare supermarket till receipts

## Lesson guidance

This lesson is largely preparation and practice in database set up. Some important database planning activities take place that will have further application in the final unit so it is advantageous if the lessons are well learned. It is probable that two or possibly three sessions will be needed to cover all the practical activities outlined here. However, if time is short, concentrate on *Activities 2* and *3.*

### Starter

In the starter, students take a general look at how computer crime might affect the operation of the supermarket. During the class session ensure they

have included the ideas of damage to or loss of data, possible theft of money if wages are misdirected and the possible suspension of business if the EPOS systems are damaged.

### Development

For *Activity 1*, encourage students to think about where all the information comes from in a familiar printout such as a till receipt: the loyalty card number comes from the card reader, the headings and greetings will not be part of the product database and the system clock will provide the date; the database provides product details and prices in response to the bar code number that was input.

The students set up a data table in *Activity 2. Worksheet 25* helps them, assuming they are using Microsoft *Access*. There are many advantages to be gained from standardising on this, but if other software is used, the instructions will have to be modified. Students enter some data, some of which can be taken from the till receipts. Card numbers will have to be invented. Allow time for this data entry; it will probably take quite a long time.

The students then, in *Activity 3*, look at just one way that the data can be sorted. In a professional database, this will not normally happen. Instead, data tend to be left alone and, instead, indexes are used to produce sorted output as and when required.

Similarly, Microsoft *Access* provides some simple menu commands for locating records. These too are rather limited in their use to simple database installations. *Activity 4* gives the opportunity to try this feature out. It is unlikely to be useful in the full-scale implementation of a big database where lots of tables and more complex enquiries are normal.

### Review

Remind students about data type considerations; this recurring theme will be revisited on page 105.

### Homework

A database wordsearch is provided on *Worksheet 26.*

## Differentiation

A lot of important technical skill is covered here. Further scope can be provided by looking at the menu options available in the Table – Datasheet view.

# Filtering and sorting data

68 | 69

## Curriculum link

**Framework coverage:** F4
**SoW:** Unit 10
**NC:** 2c, 3a
**Prior learning:** Earlier work on databases, spreadsheet experience

## Resources

- Spreadsheet software
- Text editor such as Microsoft *NotePad*
- Worksheet 27

- Worksheet 28
- Worksheet 29
- CD: CSV 2

## Lesson guidance

This general purpose lesson looks at ways that data can be transformed and manipulated, and one common data file format: CSV. Some more practical skills are covered.

### Starter

Sorting data is a common data-processing operation, and students use the familiar example of school records to help them to spot why sorting is useful. When collating the variety of ideas from the whole class, use this to underline the importance of sorting as a process.

### Development

Students are next introduced to CSV files as a useful format. For *Activity 1*, students answer questions from *Worksheet 27* based on a printout of a CSV file.

In *Activity 2*, students use a text editor to look at a CSV file called *CSV 2* that contains data about supermarket products. This will demonstrate that a simple text editor cannot be used to interrogate the data and that more powerful software is needed for data processing.

For *Activity 3*, students look at alternative and more suitable software to process the data. Stress that CSV files – and hence the data in this format – can be accepted by several different software packages. *Worksheet 28* contains instructions for sorting the data in this file.

In *Activity 4*, students use the spreadsheet's autofilter feature, a very simple way of carrying out simple database operations without the need to set up a full-blown data structure. *Worksheet 29* contains the necessary instructions to learn how to use this feature.

### Review

The students have seen a variety of ways in which a spreadsheet can be used to sort and group data. In the review, they summarise what they have learned.

### Homework

This is a chance for each individual to explain the autofilter option and to demonstrate a full understanding of it. More able students can include examples of where it is useful and provide an assessment opportunity for higher level work.

## Differentiation

Students who are making quick progress should investigate the wide variety of useful jobs that can be performed by the autofilter feature.

# Queries

## Curriculum link

**Framework coverage:** F6b, F6c
**SoW:** Unit 10
**NC:** 3a, 5a
**Prior learning:** None

## Resources

- Database management software
- Worksheet 30
- Worksheet 31
- CD: CSV 3

## Lesson guidance

The search option from the menu can be used to interrogate a simple database. However, this is limited and queries are a much more versatile and powerful interrogation tool. Knowledge of queries opens up many more possibilities for future work, and the practical activities included in this lesson could take longer than just one session. *Activity 3* can be omitted if time is short.

### Starter

Suggest that students work in pairs for this activity. Often, databases are used to produce lists so this exercise can help students to focus on a common activity in database processing.

### Development

Remind students about table structure; then, in *Activity 1*, by completing *Worksheet 30*, students import a CSV file into a new database. This should demonstrate that data can be moved easily from one application to another and then processed. Tell students that the fields are separated by commas in a CSV file, and that most software can import its data.

Students then learn about queries and their advantagess. In *Activity 2*, students follow *Worksheet 31* to discover what queries can do. It is important that students understand this topic, so linger on this section. If necessary, a second session could be allocated.

In *Activity 3*, students look at a very simple way of displaying the output of a query in a word-processed document. This is quite a crude method, but it serves the purpose at this stage. In a fully developed system, the output would be to a report or an on-screen form.

### Review

Students describe the steps that they have gone through to accomplish the output described above. This is a good way to reinforce the skills learned. The students might do this as an individual exercise and compare notes as a whole group activity.

### Homework

The homework is preparation for the next lesson on mail merge.

## Differentiation

More able students can extend their use of queries to try other useful enquiries. They can set more than one condition and alter the number of fields included.

# Mail merge

72 73

## Curriculum link

**Framework coverage:** F7a, F7c
**SoW:** Unit 10
**NC:** 2a, 3a, 3b
**Prior learning:** Database and word-processing skills

## Resources

- Spreadsheet software
- Word-processing software
- Worksheet 32
- Worksheet 33
- CD: Text 2
- CD: CSV 4
- Examples of junk mail

## Lesson guidance

This practical session sets the groundwork for many future uses of mail merge. There are various ways that mail merge can be carried out, e.g. from word-processing software or DTP software. Also, the data file can be created in almost any software form, e.g. as a *Word* table, or as a database table. In this lesson, a spreadsheet is used.

### Starter

The starter looks at the results of the previous lesson's 'junk mail' homework. Ask students to try to identify what must have been in the original database.

### Development

Give students time to understand the systems flow chart in the Student Book. It is advantageous if they are able to make use of such diagrams in their project work. For *Activity 1*, students use *Worksheet 32* to look at the flow chart symbols provided with their word-processing software.

Next: the standard or 'form' letter. The students can either write one themselves in *Activity 2* or load one from disk, e.g. the one provided as file *Text 2*. If they use *Text 2*, encourage students to make sure that it is well laid out before proceeding to the next stage.

Some general principles about choosing fields for a mail merge are discussed. Then, in *Activity 3*, students load the data file *CSV 4* into their spreadsheet software, to use this as the data file for their mail merge. Stress to the students that they need to re-save this file in spreadsheet format before using it in the merge.

For *Activity 4*, students carry out the merge, referring to *Worksheet 33*, which contains the instructions for use with Microsoft *Office* software.

### Review

Encourage students to think of other uses for mail merge, such as school reports, CD and DVD labels, mailing labels or tickets to events.

### Homework

Students often show little familiarity with system flowcharts in later years, so further valuable practice in constructing such charts is given in the homework.

## Differentiation

The more able students will come up with more and inventive uses for mail merge and this can serve as an assessment opportunity to distinguish higher level work.

# Effective web use

74 75

## Curriculum link

**Framework coverage:** F1
**SoW:** Unit 11
**NC:** 1a, 1b
**Prior learning:** Internet experience for research and leisure

## Resources

- Access to the Internet
- Worksheet 34

## Lesson guidance

This unit concentrates on the Internet and provides focused activities and some theoretical knowledge to make it more substantial. Various data handling and presentation exercises are included as well.

### Starter

The wordsearch on *Worksheet 34* includes terminology for things that are needed to access the web, most of which should be familiar to students.

### Development

The *Transmitting data* panel demonstrates that the Internet is fundamentally no different from any other network, except in scale. The same issues apply with respect to data transmission and many of the component parts are the same. The section looks at data transmission rates; some students will have no difficulty with this, but for others, it may not be appropriate. In *Activity 1*, students work out a simple calculation about transmission rates. The solution is straightforward: $(56 \times 1000)/8 = 7000$ characters per second.

Methods of connection are becoming more diverse all the time. The rapid uptake of broadband is already making some comments look out of date, but the students should be aware of bandwidth issues and how they affect performance at a workstation on a connected network. For *Activity 2*, students find out how the connection is effected in their particular school. The data transmission rates may not be a straightforward issue, but Year 8 students will be able to understand some of this. Some schools have 2Mbit connections but these lead to a local authority portal that has, say, a 10Mbit onward link to the ISP. With lots of schools connected, this can lead to bottlenecks and a poor user experience. Many users find that domestic ADSL connections give a better result. There are many ramifications to this but, basically, the more bandwidth the better. Daily fluctuations are the result of traffic volume. This may be when lots of schools log on to an LEA site at the same time or it may be due to the US 'waking up' round about lunch time in the UK! These all make interesting discussion points for the students.

In a school, there is a lot of competition for bandwidth. Point out that selfish use of the Internet, especially using it to play online games, is likely to affect the work of others. Schools need to have very clear policies about appropriate use of bandwidth. For *Activity 3*, students look at general matters of responsibility when using a shared resource. The students should already be aware of the danger of viruses and the huge amount of undesirable material that is available.

Children can face special problems when talking to others on the Internet. In *Activity 4*, students are made to think clearly and sensibly about their own personal safety when 'chatting' or sending e-mails. Any ideas for obscuring one's real identity are worth discussing.

Many students use the Internet to look things up for lessons and assignments. They should by now understand that because of the vast amount of material, printing is also a matter that requires thought. In doing *Activity 5*, students should become aware that there is a real cost and environmental problem in thoughtless and wasteful printing, and be more careful in future. However, printing restrictions may need to be enforced for those that are not as sensible.

### Review
Emphasise the main issues involved with sensible Internet use. Students should not have difficulty in understanding these and recalling them.

### Homework
The homework revises the resources needed for Internet access. It would be good if the students could explain the function of each component mentioned.

## Differentiation
Higher-level assessment often hinges on looking at matters from someone else's point of view. More able students could write Internet use policies for different groups of people.

# Facts or opinions?

| 76 | 77 |

## Curriculum link
**Framework coverage:** F1a, F1b
**SoW:** Unit 11
**NC:** 1b, 1c
**Prior learning:** Work on the Internet in Year 7 (F2–F6: Book 1 pp. 16–27)

### Resources
● Access to the Internet
● Worksheet 35

## Lesson guidance
The main curriculum link here is: 'How much do we trust material that we find on the Internet?' This lesson and the next focus on using the Internet to find out how mobile phones work and to discover the concerns about health related to mobile phone use.

### Starter
The starter looks at the differences between facts and opinions. This idea was covered extensively in Year 7 (Student Book 1, page 19), but students will benefit from reinforcement so that it isn't forgotten. The fact list ought to contain things that are demonstrably true or the informed opinions of experts; the opinions should contain things that could be argued either way. This is an important and fundamental aim of all education – to equip students with the ability to think for themselves and to realise that 'facts' are not always what they are supposed to be.

### Development
The *Mobile phones* panel introduces a potentially controversial issue: 'Do mobile phones damage your health?' Of course, no one knows the answer at the moment but there are divided opinions about it. The session starts with a few facts: the basic principles of mobile phone technology are laid out, plus the incontrovertible truth that using a mobile phone exposes the brain to radio frequency radiation. In *Activity 1*, students look at the extent to which this issue is discussed in the media.

For *Activity 2*, students find out the location of base stations. Most are clearly visible and so the students ought to be able to locate some of the nearby examples. Take this opportunity to have fun by importing a map from a map Internet site and marking the known base stations on it using graphics or word-processing software.

The amount of energy emitted by a particular phone at a particular time may affect whether it is a health hazard. For citizens to make an informed decision on this issue, they need to have access to the relevant data. In *Activity 3*, students find out how easy or difficult it is to find what you need to know, using the Internet.

Some manufacturers do give information about the energy output of their products; other sites may gloss over such concerns. In *Activity 4*, students examine the issue of bias; *Worksheet 35* encourages them to think about the partiality of any given website.

### Review
Students need to think about how reliable a source of information might be. They may think that academic sites are reliable and impartial. They may think that publicly funded bodies such as the BBC are. This may – or may not – be the case, so they

have to make judgements about how much to trust information sources, whatever the medium by which they are delivered.

### Homework
Students need to list companies in the mobile phone business. There are plenty, so a quick search with Google, Yahoo or some other search engine will produce a substantial list.

## Differentiation
Extension activities could be concerned with making judgements about websites covering news stories. Students could try to find examples of sites where there is a definite bias to one point of view. This could be used as a higher-level assessment opportunity.

# Narrowing your search    78 | 79

## Curriculum link
**Framework coverage:** F1b, F1c
**SoW:** Unit 11
**NC:** 1b, 4b, 4d
**Prior learning:** Web-based work in Year 7 (F2–F6: Book 1 pp. 16–27)

## Resources
- Word-processing software
- Access to the Internet

## Lesson guidance
This lesson continues the theme of judging whether a source is likely to be reliable. It also includes some technical material about mobile phones to add some more interest.

### Starter
The starter recalls material worked with in Year 7. Students should remember some of the more well-known domain suffixes such as .ac.uk, .com, .gov, and .edu. Some may recall the indicators of a country such as .fr, .de and .ie.

Suggest that students add some of these to their glossaries, together with the term 'domain name suffix'.

### Development
For *Activity 1*, students should quickly identify the many news providers available on the web. Every newspaper, national or local, throughout the world has something available. So, there is lots of scope for examining a wide variety of sources, and no need to restrict the search to UK providers. US or Australian news sites often have an entirely different angle on the news that is worth viewing.

For *Activity 2*, students return to the BBC website, which is well organised and very user friendly. The object of this activity is not so much to find out information, but to see how easy it is to look up what is needed from the archives and just how much information is available. Stress that altering

the search string slightly can be very helpful in narrowing down the search for useful material.

Often, the web is used to find quite specific facts, such as scientific facts and definitions. For *Activity 3*, students search for specific facts; using the terms as key words for Google should lead them to the information they require.

In *Activity 4*, students ought to notice that there is no benefit in including words such as 'of' or 'the'. The example site quoted has the .gov.au suffix which the students might guess as being that of the Australian government. The students need to consider how trustworthy this site is. Some government sites are concerned with helping their citizens; others lean more to propaganda and spin. Surfers have to judge for themselves which are which. The other site mentioned is a handset manufacturer. Again, it is a good idea if the students express their expectations first, and then visit the site to see if their expectations are confirmed.

### Review
The students can clarify what they have learned by making a list of what they consider to be useful indicators of a website's reliability.

### Homework
It is so easy to waste time and follow blind alleys when looking for information on the web. The students should have some good ideas by now of how to find what they want efficiently. Their ideas are the basis of this homework,

## Differentiation
Some subjects are much easier to research on the Internet than others. It all depends on how much the different sources are motivated to put the material on the web. More able students could list 'easy' and 'difficult' topics to research and comment on why there is a difference. This would provide an opportunity for higher-level assessment.

# Search techniques    80 | 81

## Curriculum link
**Framework coverage:** F4, F5
**SoW:** Unit 11
**NC:** 1b, 1c, 5d
**Prior learning:** Year 7 Internet topics (F5: Book 1 p. 21) and some database experience

## Resources
- Database management software – the worksheet assumes Microsoft *Access*
- Access to the Internet
- Worksheet 36
- CD: CSV 5

## Lesson guidance
This lesson makes the link between searching for material on the Internet and searching for it in a large local database. Students should recognise that similar approaches can be used.

## Starter

This focuses on what can be done with a database. The students should suggest general processes such as sorting, searching, adding, deleting and amending.

### Development

AND and OR can be used to alter the number of hits achieved in a search. In *Activity 1*, students try the effects of the examples given in any search engine and should find many more hits when they use OR.

When using several words as key words, the search engines make assumptions about whether the user wants AND or OR. The use of quote signs is introduced. In *Activity 2,* students should notice the helpful hints on how to do searches that are displayed on the search engine websites. Recommend that although students may not bother reading these hints because they are busy concentrating on where they want to go, it is worth having a look at these tips to save time later.

For *Activity 3*, students load a CSV file of weather data: *CSV 5*. Students will use this to conduct searches in a similar way to how an Internet search engine is used. *Worksheet 36* guides the students through the process. They should already know how to conduct a query using database management software.

In *Activity 4*, students continue to work on *CSV 5* answering a series of questions by means of adjusting the query. Recommend that students try some of their own queries too.

### Review

Encourage students to think about the processes they have gone through and to compare the use of database management software with that of a search engine. Database queries are easier to customise so that individual fields can be included or excluded and used in a search or not. Also, most fundamentally, queries can be used to update the underlying data. By contrast, a search engine is read-only as far as the data are concerned.

### Homework

The homework reinforces the activities performed on the weather data. The students produce a bullet-point list of the steps they needed to take to produce subsets of data in a desired order.

## Differentiation

This is achieved by the degree of sophistication used in the queries by the students. More advanced students can save the queries they produce. They can then use them as a basis for generating reports, using the report wizard.

# Producing graphs and statistics

82 | 83

## Curriculum link

**Framework coverage:** D5
**SoW:** Unit 11
**NC:** 2a, 2c
**Prior learning:** Previous spreadsheet work

## Resources

- Spreadsheet software
- Word-processing software
- CD: CSV 5

## Lesson guidance

This lesson develops students' spreadsheet techniques, using the same large file as in the previous lesson. Students are introduced to some new functions and also learn how filtering techniques can be useful in a variety of situations where they need to find the answers to questions.

### Starter

Use this starter to reinforce the students' ability to make the right choices when choosing graph types. Often they do not think about this clearly enough and choose whatever looks 'nice' from the spreadsheet wizard. If they know how to choose properly, they will choose pie, line and bar, respectively.

### Development

Students have already met the filter feature and, in this lesson, they apply this feature to answer some specific questions. In *Activity 1*, students are given some instances where the filter is useful. They should only expect to see some general trends here.

- Filtering on pressure to be greater than, say, 1000 mb followed by 1010 mb, and then taking a look at the temperatures suggests that high pressure is not necessarily associated with sunny days.
- Filtering for wind speeds of, say, greater than 45 shows very few summer days.
- Filtering humidity at greater than 90 shows only summer days.

Tell students to write this up as a report in a word-processed document and to explain the reasoning behind each filter condition.

Spreadsheets can be used for many jobs other than those that need calculations to be performed; the Data–Sort feature is particularly versatile. For *Activity 2*, students are presented with some exercises that make use of the filter feature. Remind students to take care not to accidentally sort the header row into the rest of the data. They must also ensure that all the relevant data are highlighted first.

Functions are looked at in a little more detail than previously and the term 'parameter' is defined (more for their glossary). For *Activity 3*, students add extra rows at the bottom of the data to make use of the statistical functions mentioned (*Answers*: (a) 30°

(b) 30.18 kph (c) 56% (d) 2.61 mm (e) 32). Remind them to make sure that the functions refer to the correct ranges of data.

In *Activity 4*, students revisit graph making. They have made graphs before but here they learn how to highlight non-contiguous ranges. Encourage students to describe what they did, and what the graphs showed them that was not apparent in the raw data.

### Review

After discussing the main skills learned, encourage discussion on any difficulties that students may have had. Problems and solutions could be itemised on the board or a screen.

### Homework

To make the understanding of spreadsheet terms absolutely clear, students are asked to distinguish between a formula and a function. They should recognise that a formula is generally constructed by the user and is probably fairly simple. A function requires parameters in brackets and many functions are provided with the software itself, which saves the effort of writing your own.

## Differentiation

Extension activities can centre on the investigation of other spreadsheet functions as described in the Student Book.

## Data presentation formats

84 85

### Curriculum link

**Framework coverage:** E5a
**SoW:** Unit 11
**NC:** 1b, 2a
**Prior learning:** Spreadsheet and word-processing skills

### Resources

- Spreadsheet software
- Word-processor software
- Access to the Internet

### Lesson guidance

The remainder of this unit is concerned with collecting data and presenting it for a purpose. The mobile phone safety issue provides a suitable scenario. This particular lesson contains few new skills but requires the efficient use of skills already acquired.

### Starter

Use the starter to provoke some thought about what makes a leaflet suitable for an audience aged about 10. The leaflet is required to give advice about using mobile phones safely. Discuss general approaches but only briefly at this point.

### Development

In *Activity 1*, the students enter some simple data that shows energy absorption rates for different phones. *Activity 2* should be a very easy and quick exercise for most students who are now well practised in graph making.

The *Collecting data from websites* panel then gives guidance about extracting items from web pages. This leads, in *Activity 3*, to a quick search for a suitable phone manufacturer's website and the collection of some material from it, suitable for inclusion in the advice leaflet.

### Review

Sometimes data are easy to understand in a tabular format. The review poses this as a question and students may decide that when the quantity of data is small or when it is in some sort of order, a table may be more effective than a graph.

### Homework

Remind students that ICT sources are not the only way to find what they need. The homework gives a chance for the students to think more widely.

## Differentiation

This is a very straightforward lesson. Most students should manage it all but, for some, it may be a useful chance to perfect skills that were not properly understood in the past. An extension activity could be to find out more about SAR values.

## Fitness for purpose

86 87

### Curriculum link

**Framework coverage:** E2
**SoW:** Unit 11
**NC:** 3b
**Prior learning:** DTP and word-processing experience

### Resources

- DTP software
- Word-processing software
- Worksheet 37

### Lesson guidance

In this lesson, students look at a wide variety of communication methods, most of which are made easier because of ICT methods. They examine the reasons for making choices of medium and consider how to judge success in communication.

### Starter

Help students by clarifying the distinction between generic types of software and the well-known brand names of examples. It is important that the students know the generic terms. This exercise is best carried out on an individual basis so that each student knows the terms. Any errors or omissions are corrected in a group session.

### Development

Compromises have to be made when choosing a communication medium. Choices have to take into account cost, time required, skills available and ease of setting up. For *Activity 1*, students consider how effective each method would be and how easy it is to distribute it. *Worksheet 37* helps students to set out their thoughts on this. This activity is best carried out in pairs or as individuals.

In *Activity 2*, students focus attention on how to judge success. The original aims need to be quite specific if sensible answers are to be gained from this evaluation. Suitable questions are: Have the children understood the content of the leaflet? Are they likely to act on the suggestions?

For *Activity 3*, students make decisions as to exactly what contents are to be included in a document. Remind students to bear in mind the ages and attitudes of the intended readers.

In *Activity 4*, students compare DTP with word-processing software. This activity is best done while the students actually experiment with the functions mentioned. It could take quite a long time for some to do successfully and more than one session might be required.

### Review

Look back at approaches to the leaflet production. Produce a global class list to summarise what has been decided.

### Homework

This provides further reinforcement about understanding what different software can do. Students' lists might include graphics/image manipulation software, camera download software/drivers, scanning software/scanner drivers, operating system (probably Windows), web browser, Internet dial-up software (possibly), printer drivers, possibly spreadsheet to produce graphs.

## Differentiation

Extension work could develop *Activity 4* to look at other features that are available in both DTP and word-processing software. For example, templates and mail merge can be done in each.

# Further planning and DTP skills

`88 89`

## Curriculum link

**Framework coverage:** E4a, E4b
**SoW:** Unit 11
**NC:** 3b
**Prior learning:** Previous graphic and document production work

## Resources

- DTP software
- Word-processing software
- Worksheet 38
- CD: Text 3
- CD: Image 3
- A flat pack instruction sheet, duplicated for the class

## Lesson guidance

This lesson follows up ideas about layout and style, together with some practical work to learn the necessary skills.

### Starter

The discussion revolves around how much of an information leaflet should be in words and how much in graphic form. A flat pack instruction sheet can be used as an example; so many people cannot follow the sometimes obscure hieroglyphics that characterise them!

### Development

Warn students that it is very easy to slip into writing in an automatic way, without giving enough thought about techniques for communicating your message. Emphasise that style ought to be something that is adopted in a deliberate and purposeful way with clear awareness of the audience. In *Activity 1*, students look at writing styles and comment on the needs of different readers.

Design aspects are considered next. For leaflets, there are three basic layouts: single side, folded once or folded twice, as illustrated in the Student Book. In *Activity 2*, students consider these design aspects and other layout issues. This work is best done in pairs or small groups.

When there is little spare time or for those without particularly well-developed graphic design skills, there are various ways that DTP software can help. In *Activity 3*, students look at the many different basic layouts that DTP software can provide to allow a quick start and a good-looking result. Students should have some fun looking through this huge array of possibilities.

The last section looks at making the text within *Text 3* fit into a restricted space. Writers are often constrained by the amount of space that they need to fill; producing the required volume of material is therefore one of the disciplines of document production. In *Activity 4*, students use *Worksheet 38* to remind them how text flow can be achieved.

### Review

Much planning has gone into this and other documents during this course. Some students may not enjoy the planning; they just want to use the computer as soon as possible. Remind students that planning is not really optional. Lack of planning usually gives poor results; good planning should give better results.

### Homework

Students revise what should be well-understood terms. They should be able to list basic PC peripherals and add specific requirements such as scanners, cameras and colour printers.

## Differentiation

Some students could compare the virtues of producing a leaflet with a wizard with making it from first principles. Such an evaluative approach could provide assessment opportunities for higher levels.

# Making and evaluating the leaflet

## Curriculum link

**Framework coverage:** E3, E5a, E5b
**SoW:** Unit 11
**NC:** 3b
**Prior learning:** Previous document production work

## Resources

- Word-processing software
- DTP software
- Access to the Internet

## Lesson guidance

The actual production of the leaflet could easily take more than one lesson. It tends to be an enjoyable part of the work, so let students linger on it and have fun making their leaflets look as good as possible. However, if time is short, students can confine themselves to setting out one side of the leaflet with a chart, an image and some previously produced text.

### Starter

The starter looks at DTP terminology. The students ought to know each of these terms; suggest they add them to their glossaries if they haven't done so already.

### Development

Students need to spend quite a long time, either in pairs or as individuals, putting the leaflet together for *Activity 1*. They will need to assemble their resources first. Suggest that these are collected in a folder especially for the purpose. Students need to use a variety of software to complete the work. They should work strictly within the constraints that they have set themselves and the brief given in the Student Book. Remind them of the importance of checking everything on-screen before printing it out.

The students evaluate their own work and then, for *Activity 2*, produce a written evaluation of someone else's leaflet and word process their report. As always, they should make sure that their report is well presented and professional looking with no mistakes in it.

### Review

A checklist of stages gone through completes the process. To do this well, the time allowance for this lesson will need to be generous.

### Homework

The next lessons are concerned with a small project about school trips which integrates many of the skills learned earlier. This homework is to set the scene. The idea is that they will start to think about breaking problems into manageable parts.

## Differentiation

Differentiation is by outcome. There will probably be considerable differences in content, approach and overall quality between students. Extension activities for higher levels could be to adapt the leaflet for an older audience

# Project outline

## Curriculum link

**Framework coverage:** F2, F3
**SoW:** Unit 12
**NC:** 5c, 5d
**Prior learning:** Familiarity with a range of software as covered in preceding units

## Resources

- Word-processing software
- Newspapers and magazines

## Suggested web addresses

- www.ncaction.org.uk/subjects/ict/levels.htm

## Lesson guidance

For this unit, in a series of many sessions, a complete system is planned and put together. This should develop further the ability of students to see opportunities for using ICT resources, and to do this as far as possible with 'real-life' applications. To this end, in this unit, the needs of businesses are kept in mind and the familiar theme of organising school trips is chosen.

Much has been covered already and this integration exercise is also a large undertaking. So, it may not be possible for *every* student to complete *every* aspect of this system. This offers the opportunity to make use of this section as a discriminator to arrive at assessment levels. There is scope for basic, mechanical work characteristic of the lower levels, plus scope for integrated and more thoughtful work showing the critical and evaluative skills characteristic of higher levels. Visit the National Curriculum in Action site (see above) for descriptions of what characterises each level.

### Starter

Most students will have been on several school trips and will have an idea of what is involved from an organisational point of view. For the starter, they brainstorm their ideas about how to plan a trip. Suggest they consider a variety of trips so that issues of transport, accommodation, money and contact with parents are raised naturally.

### Development

After considering a few business uses of ICT, in *Activity 1*, students write an e-mail to explain how the case study company might benefit from the use of information systems. Encourage them to go beyond the bullet points already provided and to focus on the benefits for *visits4schools*.

Students then learn about the main business functions that take place in *visits4schools*. In *Activity 2*, they suggest software that is suitable for most of the tasks that are itemised here, for example, some form of database management system for the bookings, spreadsheet or accounting software for the finance, and DTP and word-processing software for the advertising. Better students will think about customising these and also extend their thinking to include web tools, photo editors and Internet connectivity software to complete the picture.

For *Activity 3,* students consider the actual tasks performed by individuals in detail. They need to deconstruct the 'big aims' into what actually needs to be done. This will make it easier to make choices and decisions.

In any well-run company, there will be links between the departments to maximise efficiency and reduce duplication of effort. For *Activity 4,* students look at this aspect of the company and think about what information could usefully be shared. In particular, the sharing of basic school details is going to be useful to most departments. Standard letters and forms could be of wide usefulness.

### Review
Having considered the actual tasks in some detail, the whole class can review the scenario by assigning software and IT processes to some tasks.

### Homework
In this lead-in for the next lesson, students gather a few company logos and start to think about how well they work. This will be looked at in more detail in the next lesson.

## Differentiation
Not all students will be able to cover everything that is suggested in detail. The more able students will think of more tasks and more ways of solving problems. Some might be able to consider data files that could be used by different pieces of software.

# Systems analysis
94 | 95

## Curriculum link
**Framework coverage:** E4a, E4b
**SoW:** Unit 12
**NC:** 3c
**Prior learning:** Previous experience of spreadsheets and Internet research

## Resources
- Word-processing software
- Access to the Internet

## Lesson guidance
This lesson places systems analysis within the context of *visits4schools*, and looks more closely at the role of the systems analyst.

### Starter
For this starter, a very quick discussion will help to reinforce terminology knowledge. Students should identify the floppy disk as the odd one out; it is a storage medium, and not a hardware device.

### Development
The first panel explains the work of the systems analyst and, in *Activity 1,* students place themselves in this role and frame some questions to gain the information they need. Questions might be designed to find out how many items might go on an invoice, what information needs to be printed, what is predetermined and what is variable, or how the numbering system works.

The Student Book presents several standard ways of acquiring software to meet the needs of a business and, in *Activity 2,* students consider these options for the case study company. This would work well in groups of two students so that they can bounce ideas off each other.

For *Activity 3,* advise students to keep their answers closely aligned with the requirements as specified. There are many features that can be cited here – such as the entry of numerical data and the use of formulae – and the list produced could be used for assessment purposes. Better students will spot the opportunities to use IF functions (loss-making trips) and standard templates to make sure that all calculations are carried out correctly.

Hardware considerations are addressed next and, in *Activity 4,* students recommend suitable hardware for a specific scenario. Encourage them to make recommendations that are sensible for *visits4schools* and, ideally, to give comparisons to try to show best value options.

### Review
A class discussion can look at the advantages of networking. By now, students should be able to identify how data can be shared, how backups and other maintenance can be centralised and how internal e-mail could all benefit the company.

### Homework
This could produce some fairly sophisticated answers – usable as higher-level indicators. Check that students realise, perhaps after the homework has been looked at, that the purpose of *any* business is to make money; their justifications should be linked to this bottom-line approach.

## Differentiation
More able students can suggest further uses for a spreadsheet in the company, thinking outside the normal 'box' of using it for calculations. They might also investigate further the hardware recommendations section and make comparisons about hardware specifications and extras offered. Higher-level assessments can be based on how well these recommendations are justified and how well the comparisons are made.

# Finance department
96 | 97

## Curriculum link
**Framework coverage:** F3
**SoW:** Unit 12
**NC:** 2c
**Prior learning:** None

## Resources
- Spreadsheet software

## Lesson guidance
This lesson develops students' use of spreadsheets yet further. It encourages deeper thinking about what they can be used for and the wide range of benefits that derive from making good use of

spreadsheets. Encourage students to 'think outside the box' and use originality in their deployment of ICT resources.

### Starter

It is easy to make mistakes when constructing formulae or when entering lots of data into a spreadsheet. Students should always watch for odd-looking results and not to take on trust all computer output. Any output that looks wrong should be checked.

### Development

Before the spreadsheet is of use, there is a need to collect the raw data. *Activity 1* could best be done individually or in pairs, and then the results quickly posted for all to see. Like all of the preparatory activities, it should not take too long so aim for a fairly fast pace.

The *How a spreadsheet can help* panel focuses attention not only on how spreadsheets can help to improve accuracy, but also on how they can produce well-formatted output. The better students should be used to taking the trouble to make their work look well presented. Take this opportunity to emphasise how important it is to make a good impression. In *Activity 2*, students are reminded that mistakes can still be made and that they ought to remember that validation checks can be built in to a spreadsheet to make sure that any data entered are reasonable. However, there will always be the potential for human error with any system.

The *Planning the spreadsheet structure* panel specifies the requirements and, in *Activity 3*, students plan the layout. Students often don't know quite what to make of this and need to have the confidence that a few boxes, labelled with the nature of what they will contain, is sufficient at this stage.

Stress that it is good practice to check what you expect before trusting computer output. Some students may not be good at handling simple arithmetic, and may need to use a calculator to work out the cost (£10.23) for *Activity 4*. However, it is instructive to see how well they can cope with practical realities such as the one given in the Student Book. You could decide whether to allow calculators but, really, the students ought to do this individually.

### Review

Do some checking of students' results. They *should* all get the same answer! If they reach it via different – but valid – routes then that's fine!

### Homework

Impress students with the need to convince Farida. Their explanations should then provide a way to assess just how well *each individual* has absorbed the lessons.

## Differentiation

This topic can be extended in lots of ways, principally by thinking of more ways of using a spreadsheet in a business. The formatting features are so powerful that a wide variety of documents can be produced to a high standard.

# Setting up the sheet  98 | 99

## Curriculum link

**Framework coverage:** D1a
**SoW:** Unit 12
**NC:** 2c
**Prior learning:** None

## Resources

- Spreadsheet software
- Worksheet 39
- Worksheet 40

## Lesson guidance

Yet more spreadsheet techniques are dealt with in this lesson. Students might not have time to complete all the activities within the time allowed. If so, they should do at least *Activities 1* and *2*.

### Starter

The 'match the words' exercise on *Worksheet 39* includes familiar terms. Suggest that students add these to their own personal glossaries if there is time.

### Development

The workbook concept is characteristic of Microsoft *Excel* and other spreadsheet programs. Point out to students that the default new spreadsheet has three sheets as shown on the tabs at the bottom of the sheets; most might never have used more than the first one. Reinforce the general principle: *never accept default names*. Meaningful names should be chosen for all the objects and files that are used. For *Activity 1*, students make these changes.

In *Activity 2*, students use *Worksheet 40* and the information provided to set up the spreadsheet. If they do not know how to refer to a different sheet in a formula and need to be shown how to cross-reference between sheets, tell students to start the formula in the appropriate cell, and then to navigate to where the data that they need in the formula are stored so that the software constructs the correct syntax for them.

For *Activity 3*, students look at protecting cells and whole workbooks. Encourage students to protect their cells and worksheets, so as to prevent accidents. Draw attention, though, to the danger of assigning a password as explained in the Student Book; this advice should be taken seriously by those who don't want to lose access to their work!

Finally, students learn how to use the spreadsheet as a template. In this case, this is a particularly useful thing to do because the same process will be applied to all the quotes that *visits4schools* produce. Tell students to save their work in the normal way and then, for *Activity 4*, to delete variable data and save the sheet as a template.

### Review

Discuss any difficulties plus ideas from some of the students on how they were able to solve their problems.

### Homework

This practice in producing documentation will prove helpful in later years for students who continue to GCSE. The instructions should be simple and, if there is time, could be tested on someone who has no experience of using templates.

### Differentiation

The spreadsheet layout given in *Worksheet 43* can be developed to make a much more presentable output for the client. Some students may like to work on that.

# Testing the spreadsheet

`100` `101`

## Curriculum link

**Framework coverage:** D4, D6
**SoW:** Unit 12
**NC:** 1c
**Prior learning:** Previous spreadsheet experience

## Resources

- Spreadsheet software
- Worksheet 41

## Lesson guidance

This lesson looks into some more detail about how errors can be made when using spreadsheet software, or indeed in other computer applications. Ideas for preventing and fixing these problems are covered.

### Starter

The equations given may seem ambiguous. Any ambiguity arises from not understanding the rules of precedence (BODMAS) which dictate that, for example, multiply and divide are done before plus and minus, and that calculations are carried out from left to right. Ignoring BODMAS rules, the answers to the first calculation could be 30 or 36 and to the second 6 or 9.5, depending on the order in which the operations were carried out.

Explain that spreadsheets do calculations and evaluate expressions like these according to their rules of precedence. So, a spreadsheet would produce the second answer in each case. Brackets can be used to force the intended order; so $(2 + 3) \times 6$ gives the result of 30.

### Development

One strategy for testing a spreadsheet or any other software is to input valid and invalid data. If the software is set up correctly, invalid data should be rejected. Inventing suitable test data for software is an art in itself and many people are employed by software companies to do just that. For *Activity 1*, students invent some valid data to work with the spreadsheet produced in the previous lesson.

It is usual to check some calculations by hand, or using a calculator, before placing trust in a spreadsheet model. In *Activity 2*, students investigate

some deliberate errors on *Worksheet 41* and decide what should be done about them.

The concept of validation is explored next. In *Activity 3*, students work individually or in pairs to detect errors according to the rules given. Not all the rules are relevant to this example.

There are plenty of ways to use a spreadsheet to enhance presentation and *Activity 4* gives students an opportunity to experiment with a few of the effects described in the Student Book.

### Review

Encourage students to think more about rules that will help to reduce input errors. A global list can then be compiled and made available to them.

### Homework

The homework encourages the students to think about *how* the layout and presentation of the spreadsheet would be of value. More able students might mention clarity and drawing attention to the main items rather than just listing effects.

## Differentiation

There is plenty of scope to explore the presentation effects that are introduced in *Activity 4*.

# The bookings department

`102` `103`

## Curriculum link

**Framework coverage:** D7b
**SoW:** Unit 12
**NC:** 5c
**Prior learning:** Previous experience with setting up databases

## Resources

- Worksheet 42

## Lesson guidance

This is the first of four lessons on databases; students look at some general database issues before producing one in the next lesson.

### Starter

Suggest that students work individually to complete the crossword on *Worksheet 42*; it should remind them of some database terms.

### Development

Students should, by now, be able to see ways in which a database can help in some clearly defined situations. In *Activity 1*, students suggest ways in which a database could solve particular problems as described in the Student Book. This activity might work best and be more productive if students work in small groups; alternatively prompt them in a class question-and-answer session. Check that their suggestions include these advantages:

- Stored data are available to all.
- Data are less likely to be lost.
- Data are more likely to be up to date.

- Data can be interrogated in many ways.
- Searches can be carried out quickly.
- Lots of different uses can be made of the date facility.

From this activity ensure that students have a permanent record, and some fairly specific answers recorded, not just vague generalities.

The *Needs analysis* panel gives the specific processing requirements and, in *Activity 2*, students decide on the data to be stored. This is effectively the production of a list of fields. If they can be categorised under particular entities such as students, schools, bookings, coach firms and venues, then so much the better.

In *Activity 3*, students think about data types. A list of some of the more common ones is given in the Student Book. As far as possible, encourage students to decide on appropriate data types. You may want to introduce other types at this stage.

The increased reliance placed on computer-stored data can lead to vulnerability. Make sure students are aware of some of the main hazards involved in storing data and how these can be minimised. Apart from having backups, there should be measures in place to prevent deletions in the first place. For *Activity 4,* students may suggest ways of limiting access to files or parts of files or making some files read-only. If they miss this as an option, give them a brief description.

### Review

The need for backing up can be made more relevant to the students by looking at their own work. Ask them to consider just how far back they would be prepared to go to repeat work that was lost. Check that they are aware that the backup tapes should be kept away from the computer, preferably off site.

### Homework

Reasons for being careful about data can be included in the homework. A few rules would be expected too, such as logging out of workstations when not using them and keeping passwords secure.

## Differentiation

Further work on data types can be given to students who require extension activity. They could speculate on what problems there might be if the wrong data type were assigned to a field, such as making a field for money a text field.

# Database implementation

104 105

## Curriculum link

**Framework coverage:** F2, D3
**SoW:** Unit 12
**NC:** 1c
**Prior learning:** Previous experience with setting up databases

## Resources

- Database software, such as Microsoft *Access*
- Worksheet 43

## Lesson guidance

Students may require more than one lesson to complete the activities. It is advantageous to allow for this but *Activities 1* and *2* are prerequisites for the following lessons.

### Starter

As a lead-in for this starter, explain to students the concept of a paperless office. This idea is not new and is almost certainly a forlorn hope, but there are aspects of it that are feasible. During a brief discussion, students might consider how much people want to have paper to take away and study at their leisure.

### Development

Students need to set up a database table. You may be wary of using Microsoft *Access* at this stage but, even with low ability groups, it can work very well; it just requires a good understanding of where the work is leading and what needs to be achieved. Simple educational alternatives to *Access* do not generally prepare students for future database work.

Explain to students that using a relational database management system like Microsoft *Access* involves the handling of lots of 'things' or objects (such as tables, forms and reports). These 'things' can be seen in Design view or a 'working' view – you are either making them or using them – and you can easily switch between these two views. A database has to have at least one table, and so, in *Activity 1*, students set up a table from the fields already decided on. This table needs a primary key; so, introduce the basic database concept of a primary key straight away. It need not be a problem: any entity or 'thing' needs a unique reference number to distinguish it from other similar 'things'. A school name is no good as a key because many schools may have the same name. A number can always uniquely identify a 'thing'. Thus a reference number is always a suitable primary key.

*Access* is fussy about setting up primary keys and tries to be helpful if you try to save a table without setting one field as the primary key. It is poor practice to let the software make decisions for you; encourage students to make explicit decisions about a primary key so that everything is under their control.

While doing *Activity 1*, students can use the description field to make notes about what they are doing. Encourage the use of comments when setting up a system; it does not affect functionality and since you always forget what your thinking was after a while, comments act as a reminder. Advise students that, when setting up an *Access* database, they should not accept the default file name of db1. Instead, they should enter a meaningful name. At this stage, students could enter the details of a few schools into the data table to make the report look more realistic but, in *Activity 2*, there are more data to be put in, so they can wait till then.

For *Activity 2*, students set up a form using a wizard, and then enter data on *Worksheet 43*. Explain that a form is one object that is best set up with a wizard, ready for customising in design view. Explain also that data entered using a form automatically update the underlying data table.

Then, for *Activity 3*, students use a wizard to produce a report. Stress that there are wizards available for setting up lots of different things in *Access*, not just reports, and that wizards are available in many other software packages. Recommend that students use wizards when a quick and easy fix is wanted, but not when a large degree of customisation is required. Often, wizards provide a good way to start a design but then need to be followed by more detailed 'tweaking'. Microsoft *Access* reports are generally best made with wizards at this level, but not tables. Tell students only to use them when instructed to do so.

### Review
The students list outputs in the form of reports in the context of the scenario. They can work in pairs for this and share ideas afterwards.

### Homework
By now, the students should understand how to use wizards and be able to describe the advantages of using them.

## Differentiation
More able students will be able to compare the advantages with the drawbacks of using wizards. There is also scope for customising the objects in this section. For example, the form can be greatly enhanced in terms of fonts, colours and layouts.

# Testing the database  106 107

## Curriculum link
**Framework coverage:** F6a, D2
**SoW:** Unit 12
**NC:** 1c
**Prior learning:** Earlier units

## Resources
- Database software, such as Microsoft *Access*

## Suggested web addresses
- **www.royalmail.co.uk/quick_tools/postcodes/ default.htm**

## Lesson guidance
The importance of accuracy is again examined. Then, students have practice in setting up and running queries. Emphasise the importance of testing.

### Starter
Remind students of the importance of accuracy in the success of a business. Check that students understand that testing is designed to break a system – not just to 'see that it works'. A good test is one that discovers a fault not found by other testing. Stress that it is best that someone other than the

software developer does the testing.

### Development
Check that students understand that data verification is at least partly a human check on data to make them as accurate as possible. In *Activity 1*, students look at just one way in which address details can be checked. The relevant website is listed above.

For *Activity 2*, students make a query or queries. They should already know how to do this, but allow some time for a reminder. Queries are best made manually in design view because the wizard may lead to poor choices being made.

*Activity 3* provides a further example of testing. The need for a look at the complete data table followed by a query run is a good example of how systems should be tested against expected outcomes. Check that students know that just doing a test run without clear expectations cannot help much in determining whether the system is working as required.

The students have had some practice in setting up reports. In *Activity 4*, they make reports to match exactly given requirements. This may take some students quite a long time, so allow time for this.

### Review
Ask students which report format they used and how they came to their decision.

### Homework
Students explain why testing is needed. Higher-level assessments can be based on how well students appreciate the need of businesses for accuracy and reliability in their software.

## Differentiation
Students who cope well with this work can be pushed further; ask them to compare the benefits of using reports and queries so as to find out what is required. They should discover that reports are best for printed output but queries are more versatile.

# Mail merge  108 109

## Curriculum link
**Framework coverage:** F4, F5
**SoW:** Unit 12
**NC:** 3a, 3b
**Prior learning:** Word-processing and data-management skills

## Resources
- Word-processing software
- Database software

## Lesson guidance
This straightforward skills-building lesson concentrates on mail merge. Mail merge has many potential applications in schoolwork and it is useful to practise it from time to time.

### Starter
Help the students' discussion of the reasons for using mail merge in this instance towards the idea of targeted marketing. Those schools already in the

database are likely to be interested in the promotional material. The mail-merge process can be selective so that only those schools required are targeted.

### Development

For *Activity 1*, students consider the advantages of mail-merged letters. This should allow the students, preferably on their own or in pairs, to suggest some other business uses, e.g. invoice reminders, invoices themselves and booking confirmations.

The Student Book shows a system flow chart for the mail-merge process. For *Activity 2*, students compare it with one they looked at earlier (page 73). The difference is that a query in database software has been used.

The next stage is to set up a form letter; this is the term used in Microsoft *Word* to describe the source document, i.e. the letter that is to be duplicated to a number of recipients. For *Activity 3*, students produce the letter and set out what data need to be inserted. You may decide to combine *Activities 3* and *4* and to add the merge fields once the connection has been made to the Microsoft *Access* query.

### Review

Take this opportunity to discuss any problems, and to share ideas of how they can be dealt with.

### Homework

The next lesson looks at company logos, so the students need to collect some.

## Differentiation

There are opportunities in the mail-merge operation to experiment with conditional merges. If time allows, students could look at the use of the word processor to produce mail-merged mailing labels.

# Designing the logo     110 111

## Curriculum link

**Framework coverage:** F7b
**SoW:** Unit 12
**NC:** 3a
**Prior learning:** Use of graphics software as Book 1 p. 41

## Resources
- Some well-known logos projected onto a screen
- Worksheet 44
- Graphics software

## Lesson guidance

Company logos provide a good excuse to introduce material on graphic software; students also have fun in designing their own. They provide a nice link with real life and everyone can have an opinion on them.

### Starter

The wordsearch – *Worksheet 44* – is about various company and IT themes that have relevance to this project.

### Development

Ask students why companies have logos; they should easily identify the need for a corporate image. Many logos are based on initials printed in fancy fonts – ask students for opinions on that approach. Logos are notoriously expensive to produce and some are memorable. For *Activity 1*, students note down how effective certain logos are and suggest how they work. Take this opportunity to encourage a free-ranging discussion. To add interest, you might ask students for examples of logos that have flopped, and consider why this was the case.

The *Features of logos* panel distinguishes between a slogan and a logo. Tell students that all sorts of messages can be put across in a well-designed logo and that some companies jealously guard their rights to reproduce them. Many logos are accompanied by slogans. These are often prominent in schools and public sector organisations such as the LAPD's 'To protect and to serve'. For *Activity 2*, students consider how a slogan differs from a logo.

Graphics software was covered in Year 7, but here the focus is on the implications of vector versus bit-mapped images. For *Activity 3*, students need to find out which graphics packages there are available to them in the school.

The logo for *visits4schools* is then specified. In real-life, more constraints would be placed on the design company. Here, students are given sufficient restriction to give *Activity 4* a focus but with enough freedom for them to have fun. This section will probably be the longest to actually execute and the students could work individually or in pairs. Nonetheless, to leave time for a brief review, the students will need to work quickly.

### Review

Briefly review the activities of the lesson. Give some consideration to whether some of the logos produced do what is required. They could be projected onto a screen for discussion.

### Homework

There is a self-evaluation exercise for each student. In addition, students need to collect some flyers as preparation for the next discussion.

## Differentiation

If required, students could make vector and bit-mapped versions of their logo and compare them for graininess and scalability.

# Making a flyer     112 113

## Curriculum link

**Framework coverage:** E5a
**SoW:** Unit 12
**NC:** 3a
**Prior learning:** Experience of using graphics, DTP and word-processing software

## Resources
- DTP software
- Word-processing software
- Graphics software

- Flyers and advertisements from previous homework

## Lesson guidance

This lesson practises skills that have already been developed. It should pose no problems and should take very little time to complete.

### Starter

The different ways of advertising are briefly listed, such as newspaper adverts, magazines, websites, television, radio, cinema, posters on walls, on buses and trains, on F1 cars, football players' shirts and so on. Ask students where computers fit in with each type of advertising identified.

### Development

For *Activity 1*, students decide what needs to be on a flyer. Given enough examples of flyers, students should be able to work out what is essential information. If any of the flyers have been produced by amateurs, this may provide a good opportunity to illustrate what not to do.

For *Activity 2*, students prepare a draft copy of their flyer – this can be done with pencil and paper or roughly set out using drawing tools. Make sure that students include all relevant detail.

Students then turn to identifying where the flyers will go. In *Activity 3*, students should identify the town or postcode field of a database as appropriate to target a particular area. Some students will realise that, to target secondary schools, an extra field will be needed in the data table to hold that detail.

In *Activity 4,* the flyer is made. Ideally, this should be an individual exercise, and enjoyable for most, even though combining text and graphics has been well practised before. There is scope for experimenting and many students will want to spend some time perfecting their leaflets.

### Review

A paired activity forms the review and the focus should be on how the finished product meets the initial requirements, not just on impact or aesthetics.

### Homework

The evaluation is on an individual basis. The homework can be focused on the company's response; one way of doing this would be to produce a letter, as if from the company, commenting on the finished product.

## Differentiation

The more able students could discuss the choice of software to produce the leaflet and give reasons for their choice.

# An itinerary

## Curriculum link

**Framework coverage:** E4a, E4b, E5a
**SoW:** Unit 12
**NC:** 3a, 3b
**Prior learning:** Earlier work in this unit

## Resources

- Word-processing software
- Spreadsheet software
- Access to the Internet
- Worksheet 45
- Worksheet 46

## Lesson guidance

This multi-skilled lesson has a single focus – to produce an itinerary – and provides an opportunity to synthesise something new from previously learned techniques.

### Starter

*Worksheet 45* is used to sort the events during a day trip into order. It may provide some practice for those who don't fully understand the 24-hour clock!

### Development

The *What is an itinerary?* panel identifies the essential information. In *Activity 1*, students plan how the display should look. *Worksheet 46* is needed to ensure that all the information is included in the plan.

To see how useful they can be in planning any journey with maps, students could be encouraged to visit one or two of the map websites. E-mail is also considered and *Activity 2* poses a question about advantages of e-mail. Check that students have arrived at these answers:

- Speed of delivery
- Low cost of sending
- Facility to send attachments
- Ease of replying by hitting the reply button
- Automatic record keeping
- Facility to copy communications to a number of recipients

A tabulated document such as an itinerary may be sensibly produced in either word-processing or spreadsheet software. The main argument in favour of word processing would be if there were substantial amounts of ordinary text to go with the itinerary. Otherwise, a spreadsheet would seem to be a better choice because of its rich set of table formatting features and the ability to do calculations. In *Activity 3*, students go through this reasoning process; some might suggest using both items of software and embedding the spreadsheet data into a word-processed document

For *Activity 4*, students create their itineraries using information from the e-mail printed in the Student Book.

### Review

Have a general discussion of the software issues so that all students are aware of the possibilities.

### Homework

The principles of this lesson are reinforced with a new task based on the same ideas.

### Differentiation

Some students might like to make a generic itinerary spreadsheet, which is updated according to data entered in a special input area.

# Information for school staff

116 117

## Curriculum link

**Framework coverage:** E5a, E5b, D5
**SoW:** Unit 12
**NC:** 3b
**Prior learning:** Presentation software skills from Year 7 (E5b, E5c: Book 1 p. 28)

## Resources

- Presentation software, such as Microsoft *PowerPoint*
- Microsoft organisation chart – available in the object library

## Lesson guidance

The emphasis in this lesson is on synthesis, with opportunities taken to add a few new skills as well as revising old ones. There are also opportunities to highlight a few extra features of the software.

### Starter

From the many presentations done in Year 7, students should be able to recall some of the basic rules of presentations: clarity, simplicity, not too much on each slide, not too many fonts and care with colour contrasts.

### Development

*Visits4schools* sends a representative to the school to give a presentation about the company, for reasons as itemised in the Student Book. For *Activity 1*, students can work in pairs or on their own to organise these ideas into about 6 slides. Check that each slide focuses on a single idea.

Some students may already be familiar with using an organisation chart. As a reminder for them and to introduce organisation charts to other students, *Activity 2* requires students to use this excellent utility. Useful additions or applets like this are available from a common library accessible through any component of the Microsoft *Office* suite. Warn students that because an organisation chart can spread widely and not fit on a page, they need to take care in that respect. However, the finished chart is embedded into the application document as a graphic so it can be resized if necessary. It can be updated whenever required by double clicking on it.

Slide masters offer an easy way to provide consistency throughout a presentation, and in *Activity 3*, students add the name of the school on the slide master so that it will appear on every slide.

Another useful applet available throughout Microsoft *Office,* the chart builder, provides a simple template of a typical chart and lets the user adapt it according to individual needs. In *Activity 4*, students experiment with using this.

### Review

As well as quickly recapping the skills looked at, the review asks for comparisons to be made with using a spreadsheet to produce a chart. Students' answers should recognise how spreadsheets give more control and have far more options, but accept that the applet is readily available for a small and simple job. Throughout the entire course, students should be learning what tools are best suited to what jobs and that, often, it is a matter of personal preference.

### Homework

In Year 7, students wrote speaker notes to go with a presentation. Here they do so again, but stress that the emphasis must be on a short, punchy approach suited to an audience of teachers. Assessment issues here are whether the script is indeed well aimed at the intended audience.

## Differentiation

The lesson is not really about producing a particularly refined presentation, rather to try new techniques. Extension work could be to refine the presentation and perhaps to include some multimedia effects.

# Starting a website

118 119

## Curriculum link

**Framework coverage:** E1, E2
**SoW:** Unit 12
**NC:** 3c
**Prior learning:** Previous work in the Year 8 course

## Resources

- Spreadsheet software
- Word-processing software
- CD: Spreadsheet 5

## Lesson guidance

Continuing the theme and using it as a vehicle for always introducing new knowledge and ideas, some more website issues are explored.

### Starter

Websites that succeed generally have a clear purpose. Encourage free-ranging discussion about why certain organisations have sites. Often a website is 'expected'; a company without a website stands out as in some way deficient. Still, the underlying purpose should be clear if the best use is to be made of the site.

### Development

For *Activity 1*, students focus on why *visits4schools* might benefit from a website. Remind students that the purpose of any business is to make money so they should be asking how a website could help in that respect. A web presence should make *visits4schools* more visible and there is always the possibility that schools might want to leave details on its site so that they are informed of new offers or destinations. Ease of booking may encourage more customers, but a worldwide presence might not relevant to this company.

The Student Book then offers ideas about what could go on the site. In *Activity 2*, students add to this list. Suggestions might include: a history of the company, where it is located and maybe pictures of the staff.

The likelihood of students recommending *visits4schools* is raised as a way of attracting new business. Emphasise how important it is to tailor things to suit an audience. Then, in *Activity 3*, students suggest ways of tailoring the *visits4schools* site so as to appeal to students, e.g. to have a 'busy' feel to it with lots of colour, animation, sound and images.

Security is always a problem to be addressed with online facilities. The *Security and the web* panel introduces encryption, which could be time-consuming. The example, *Spreadsheet 3*, shows how a message can be encoded simply. For *Activity 4*, students type in a message and look at the formulae and functions to see how the encryption works.

### Review

Review any issues that students raise, but focus on what different students suggest for website ideas so that it can feed into the next lesson.

### Homework

Understanding of encryption is tested and developed in the homework. This could go as deep as the students want and could form a useful vehicle for assessment of higher-level work, especially if awareness is shown of how encryption is an essential part of conducting business over the Internet.

## Differentiation

Students who are working quickly can explore encryption further. The example spreadsheet can be much improved to produce less 'crackable' code and the interface could also be improved.

# Planning and setting up the website

120 121

## Curriculum link

**Framework coverage:** E3
**SoW:** Unit 12
**NC:** 3a, 3c
**Prior learning:** None

## Resources

- Web-browser software
- Word-processing software
- Access to the Internet

## Lesson guidance

Students' ideas for the *visits4schools* website feed into the planning done in this lesson. The emphasis is on learning some theoretical aspects of websites and the associated knowledge, so the website is not created in this sequence of lessons. However, if time allows, it could be implemented.

### Starter

Discuss the business sense of allowing Internet bookings; there are many advantages of using e-commerce. Stress however, that some people, for various reasons, do not want to use the Internet to conduct business, so it might be foolish to discontinue 'traditional' methods.

### Development

For *Activity 1*, students need only briefly look at the evaluation criteria for the finished site. You could conduct this as a class question-and-answer session. Remind students that, without evaluation criteria, it is impossible to judge whether a finished product is a success.

*Activity 2* provides students with further practice in producing a site map, for the *visits4schools* website. Encourage students to set up folders; explain that this is good practice and shows essential organisational skills.

Students need to develop their skills in using the web for research. For *Activity 3*, students need to find out about web-authoring packages on the market, some of which are available free or on a trial basis. Often, the best deals are on the web and there is certainly a much bigger marketplace than is available in the physical neighbourhood. Using Google, the key phrase *web authoring software* will produce many suitable links.

The *Setting up the site* panel raises an economic issue: the cost of a site may be based on its size. For *Activity 4*, students explain how size can be minimised by choosing suitable graphic file formats. For further information on file sizes, see page 32.

### Review

Take this opportunity to revise the software available for web authoring. Remind students that text editors have their place, and that the more sophisticated packages have WYSIWYG and site management capability. They also can automate many of the more elaborate effects that would otherwise take quite a lot of effort with the HTML code.

### Homework

This homework may appeal most to those with some artistic creativity. For others, looking at other similar websites could be a good starting point.

## Differentiation

More able students can produce some comments on the advantages of shopping on the Internet and produce some further product comparisons.

# Testing the website

`122` `123`

## Curriculum link
**Framework coverage:** E7
**SoW:** Unit 12
**NC:** 3b, 3c
**Prior learning:** Earlier units

## Resources
- Web-browser software
- Access to the Internet

## Suggested web addresses
- **www.google.com/addurl.html**
- **www.diy.com**
- **www.theaa.com**

## Lesson guidance
More website issues are explored here, as well as some further thoughts on testing.

### Starter
This starter revises work done in Year 7, plus what is undoubtedly general knowledge. Stress that choosing key words that work involves putting in enough words to narrow down the search but not so many as to prevent a match. Remind students of the use of AND and OR to widen or narrow a search.

### Development
Accuracy has been stressed at many points in this unit. For *Activity 1*, students offer practical suggestions about checking for accuracy on a website. This will largely be *verification* of content rather than *validation*, i.e. it will be human checks against the original source material. Recommend asking for a second opinion; this should help to ensure that no mistakes are missed.

A website might work very well on the computer where it was developed, but have problems once it is released to the world. There may be problems of file name incompatibilities and the directory structure must match that of the source machine. All the resources such as the graphics files must be in place and in the location that the HTML expects. Most users have Microsoft *Internet Explorer*, but significant numbers use Netscape *Navigator* so these eventualities need testing too. In *Activity 2*, students consider how to correct spelling errors. Not many ISPs will allow remote editing, so these errors need to be fixed on the original machine, and then the corrected files uploaded again to overwrite the incorrect ones. Stress how important it is, therefore, to ensure 100% accuracy of content prior to uploading.

A new site needs to be noticed. Its address needs to be included in the catalogue of a search engine. Most search engines will eventually find a new site and update their databases but they search in different ways, and so it is a good idea to notify them. Students can see how to do this by visiting the Google page listed above. For *Activity 3*, students suggest words that might generate 'hits' if someone were looking for this type of service. Something like the following might result when the site is finished:

<META Name='keywords' Content='school trip excursion party bookings educational visits'>

Domain names are highly valued commodities and new suffixes such as .biz have been added to cope with the demand. Encourage students to discuss how to choose a domain name that is easy to remember but is different from names already registered. Some domain names include some ordinary words so that an association is kept. For example aa.com belongs to American Airlines so the British Automobile Association chose theaa.com. In *Activity 4*, students visit the *howstuffworks* site again to see how domain names are looked after. Tell students to make notes on a word processor from this very clear and easy to read site.

### Review
Discuss how companies cope with the obvious domain names already being registered. For example B&Q has a web domain name of www.diy.com.

### Homework
How Paul permits Internet access at work will depend on his budget and how much he trusts his staff! Many different approaches are acceptable here. Some students will talk about accessibility to different staff. The more technically minded might look up material on routers, ISPs, ISDN and DSL. There is certainly scope for assessment here!

## Differentiation
The homework provides much scope for differentiation. Extension work could be to look up some obvious domain names by typing them into the URL box and seeing if the expected owner is in fact registered to it. For most really big companies, the expected results will come up but, for local concerns, there may be some surprises.

# The final stages

`124` `125`

## Curriculum link
**Framework coverage:** D7b, E3
**SoW:** Unit 12
**NC:** 4a, 4c
**Prior learning:** Earlier units

## Resources
- Worksheet 47

## Lesson guidance
Attention switches from the website back to the main computer system that Paul wants to help him run his business. Focus is on the many practical issues that follow the installation of a system.

### Starter
There are many health and safety matters that students ought to be aware of and the starter briefly explores some of these. *Worksheet 47* has some points about health and safety. Students might like

to look at their own working environment in a new light after looking at this!

### Development

Some standard systems life cycle work is covered here. In *Activity 1*, students should identify the danger of lost data if the new system is used and the old one abandoned. If the new one has problems, there is no backup. Parallel running involves the effort of doing everything twice.

The theme of safety is revisited in *Activity 2*. *Worksheet 47* is again required for this, although books such as the excellent Letts *GCSE ICT Success Guide* could be consulted for further ideas. Encourage students to produce something that is actually usable, so stress that it needs to be punchy and easy to understand.

The *Improvement* panel discusses the maintenance phase. For *Activity 3*, students anticipate some changes that might need to be made, such as hardware or operating system upgrades, the system becoming too slow when there are a lot of data in it, and maybe the users wanting a better user interface.

The *Troubleshooting* panel discusses support: something that has to be dealt with by all computer users. Discussion of how the school organises support for its users could help students to understand what is involved. Of course all modern software has its own help facilities. In *Activity 4*, students look at a typical help system that makes use of hypertext; they can judge for themselves how easy it is to use.

### Review

The review covers the whole unit. Understanding the ways in which the listed items of software are useful in a business is a great achievement in Year 8, and may provide a good assessment opportunity because so much could have been covered.

### Homework

The conclusion is reinforced in the homework and the better students will be able to make a fair summary of how computers have helped. Those who make a good job of this can be rightly proud of their progress during Year 8!

## Differentiation

So much has been covered that there is a wealth of opportunity for differentiation by outcome and all students should be able to derive something useful out of the work.

Look at this example of a page from the Internet and then answer the questions.

GO BACK **≡Rail**Speed NEW JOURNEY

**Timetable enquiry: Heversedge to Marplebury**

**Outward journey**

Wednesday 10 September 2003

| Depart | 17:32 | 17:41 | 18:04 | 18:04 | 18:38 |
| --- | --- | --- | --- | --- | --- |
| Arrive | 20:40 | 20:46 | 21:11 | 21:17 | 21:41 |
| Changes | 0 | 1 | 2 | 1 | 0 |
| Duration | 3:08 | 3:05 | 3:07 | 3:13 | 3:03 |

EARLIER TRAIN  VIEW DETAILS  LATER TRAIN

**Return journey**

To obtain return journey times, please specify…

Return date (dd/mm/yy) [            ]

Departure time [00 ▼] [00 ▼]

GET TRAIN TIMES

**Ticket prices and availability**

Number of adults [1 ▼]   Number of children (under 16) [0 ▼]

Ticket type [Any ▼]   Return? ○ Yes ○ No

Railcard? ○ Yes ○ No   CHECK PRICES AND AVAILABILITY

**1** How many train journeys are shown?

**2** What is the date of the journey?

**3** How many journeys involve changing trains?

**4** What is the fastest journey time?

**5** Why do you think the columns showing train times are shaded?

**6** On the site, all the buttons are in the same colour. Why do you think this is?

**7** Why do you think the display only shows the times for a few train journeys?

Success for Schools: ICT – © Letts Educational 2003

Here is a wordsearch using words connected with how you present information.

| N | D | C | T | R | M | M | B | T | S | L | J | K | T | F |
|---|---|---|---|---|---|---|---|---|---|---|---|---|---|---|
| H | M | A | O | S | F | F | C | M | H | D | H | N | A | O |
| O | B | I | E | L | A | S | B | R | L | B | E | H | B | N |
| S | D | Z | D | R | O | U | J | H | F | F | F | V | L | T |
| R | I | L | V | P | F | U | S | E | L | T | I | T | E | S |
| S | G | K | O | J | S | N | R | J | F | B | A | N | S | V |
| A | W | Y | D | B | S | S | Q | Q | A | Y | H | S | Z | T |
| H | S | J | V | R | B | C | D | C | N | E | C | N | V | O |
| F | V | I | A | G | R | C | I | I | A | I | B | E | S | K |
| T | N | A | L | C | L | N | M | H | R | W | V | U | T | S |
| S | E | T | A | L | P | M | E | T | P | G | Z | Z | N | V |
| G | Y | X | V | D | W | N | D | E | B | A | H | H | E | O |
| H | E | A | D | I | N | G | S | O | F | L | R | T | D | I |
| I | T | A | L | I | C | X | S | C | F | A | X | G | N | O |
| W | G | O | W | H | E | K | S | V | L | Z | Z | E | I | G |

| | | |
|---|---|---|
| BOLD | HEADINGS | TABS |
| COLOUR | INDENTS | TEMPLATES |
| FONTS | ITALIC | TITLES |
| GRAPHICS | SIZES | |
| GRIDS | TABLES | |

# 3 Parts of a computer system

Here is a wordsearch based on the names of parts of a computer system.

| M | X | M | M | C | R | L | R | M | R | B | W | C | P | G |
|---|---|---|---|---|---|---|---|---|---|---|---|---|---|---|
| F | O | G | O | K | C | Y | L | E | W | R | X | A | K | P |
| W | W | N | V | U | E | T | N | N | E | W | K | M | I | Y |
| C | A | L | I | V | S | N | G | K | P | E | M | E | K | J |
| F | P | D | I | T | A | E | A | H | Y | M | D | R | B | F |
| A | Y | R | M | C | O | E | S | B | J | R | D | A | H | H |
| B | D | U | S | B | P | R | O | R | E | T | N | I | R | P |
| V | M | A | M | S | R | A | K | J | N | M | F | O | I | B |
| V | E | X | X | W | R | E | T | Z | G | P | C | G | O | H |
| M | M | A | R | D | W | A | T | T | J | T | E | Z | I | D |
| Q | O | B | D | A | L | K | S | O | X | Z | N | T | Y | H |
| L | R | T | D | U | K | K | Z | D | R | X | X | E | D | Y |
| S | Y | R | L | T | D | M | F | I | C | L | V | H | F | S |
| R | A | A | G | U | B | F | U | C | O | S | M | U | M | E |
| H | R | W | R | S | H | N | K | W | C | P | V | T | Z | O |

| CAMERA | HARD | DRIVE | MOUSE | SCANNER |
|---|---|---|---|---|
| MEMORY | KEYBOARD | MONITOR | PRINTER | SPEAKER |

Success for Schools: ICT – © Letts Educational 2003

Use this diagram to help you to plan for your display.

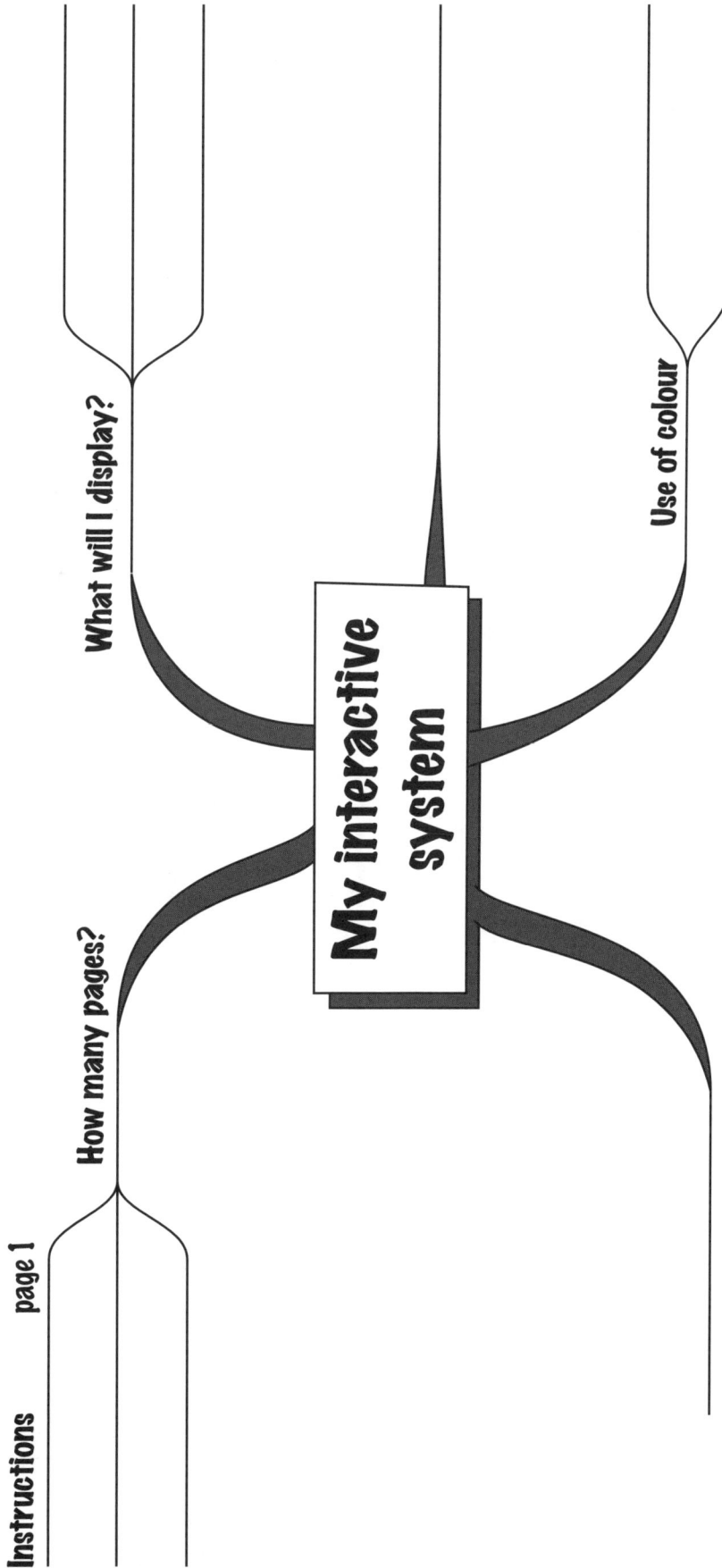

**Instructions**

**How many pages?**

page 1

**My interactive system**

**What will I display?**

**Use of colour**

Here some steps to run a bath.

- Wash
- Fill the bath with water
- Get dressed
- Empty the bath water
- Get undressed
- Get into bath
- Get out of bath

Put the steps into the right order in the flow chart.

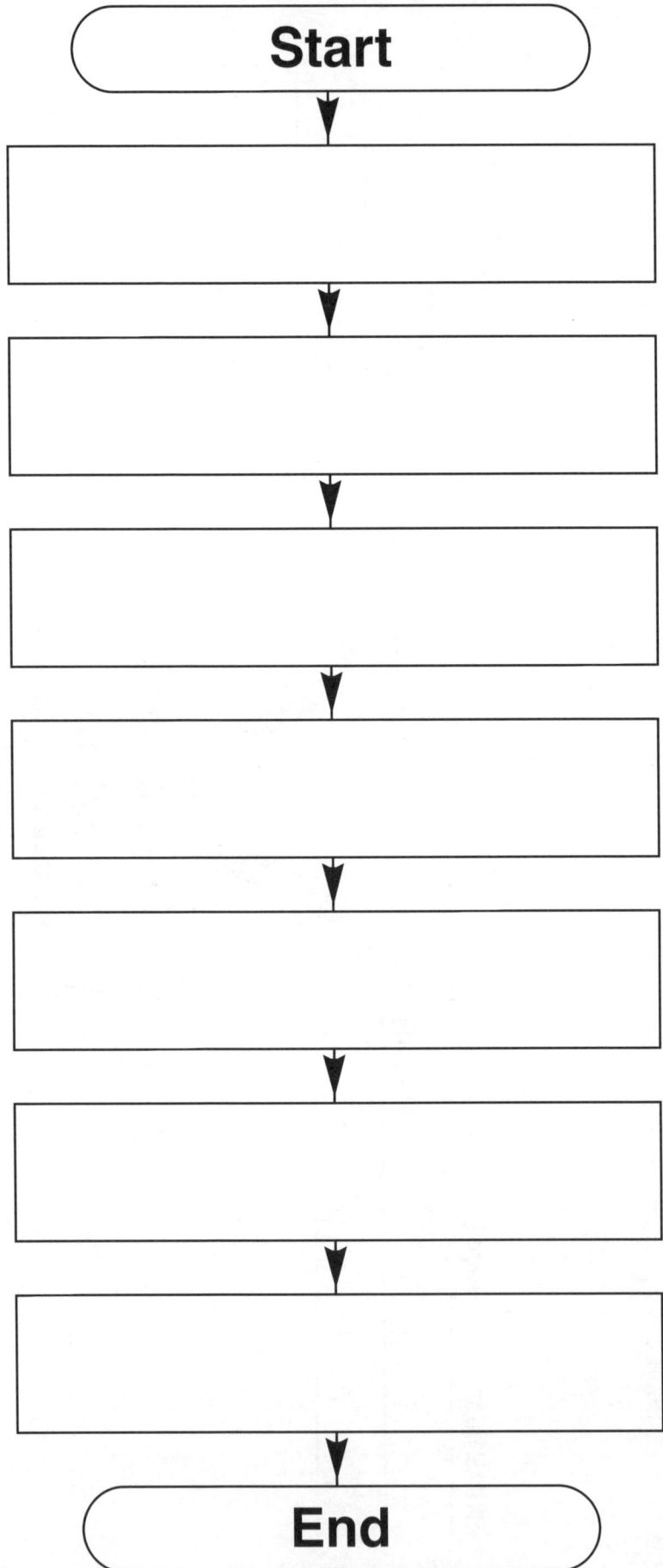

**Start**

↓

↓

↓

↓

↓

↓

↓

**End**

Using these steps, draw a flow chart in the correct order.

Display times for next train

Clear screen

Display the start screen

Finish

Start

Next train button pressed

Start again button

Place these words in the grid.

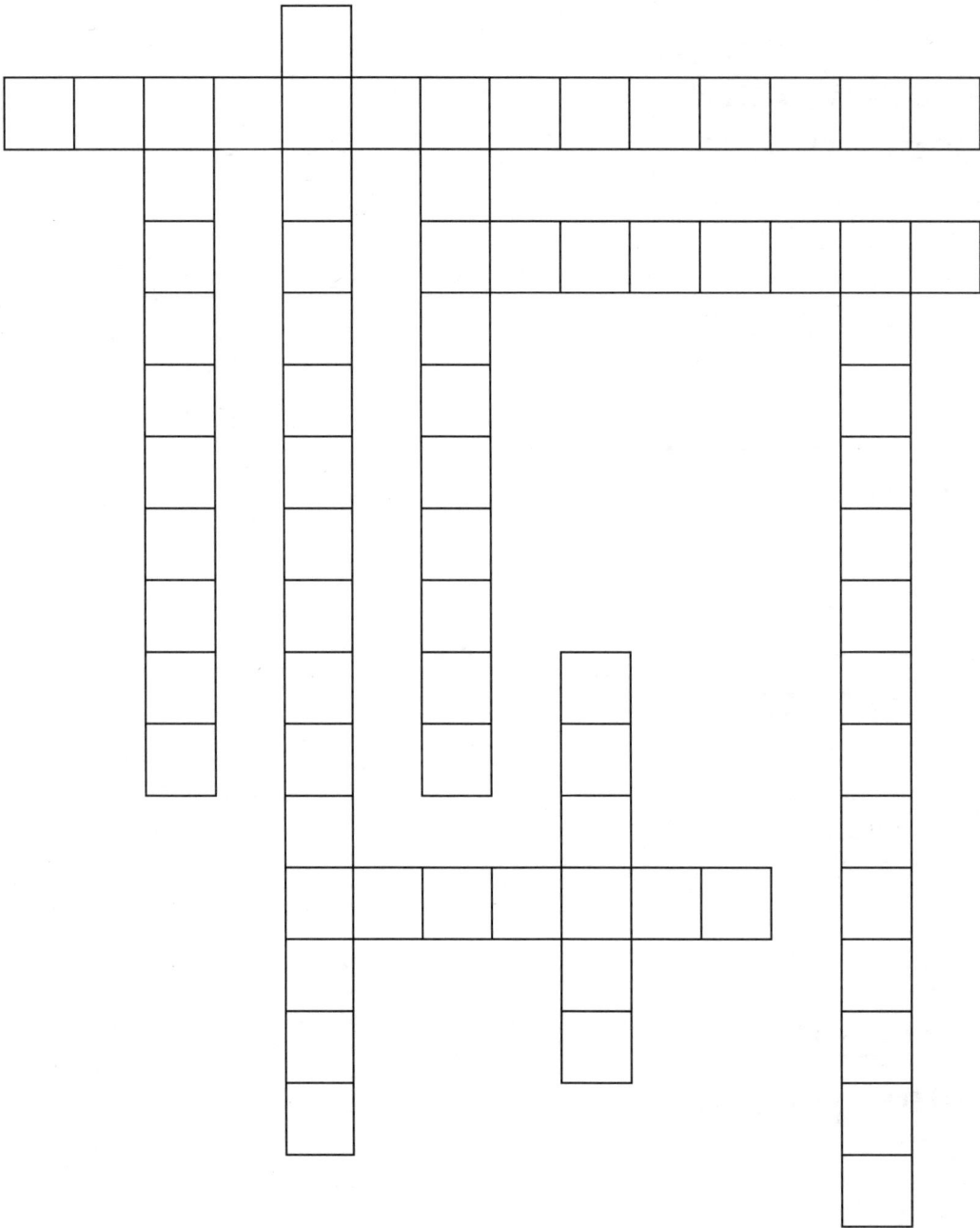

Identification       Production

Feasibility Study    Testing

Analysis             Implementation

Design               Evaluation

Match the words on the left to their correct description.

| | |
|---|---|
| browser | A link from one place to another on a web page |
| HTML | A website that holds details of many other websites and allows you to search for them using key words |
| hyperlink | Software which allows a person to view web pages |
| download | Short for uniform resource locator |
| search engine | Short for hypertext mark-up language |
| URL | Moving about on the web |
| web page | Short for the World Wide Web |
| WWW | A document on the World Wide Web |
| Navigation | To transfer data from one computer to another |

**Unit 2 Publishing on the web**

**53**

Complete this wordsearch of Internet terms.

| Z | M | L | P | S | H | N | S | U | J | I | J | B | R | W |
|---|---|---|---|---|---|---|---|---|---|---|---|---|---|---|
| I | Y | J | R | V | Y | Y | Z | E | K | E | R | V | E | M |
| L | M | N | D | N | P | L | G | K | U | O | U | R | S | O |
| D | E | J | P | I | E | D | B | D | A | D | E | L | W | D |
| D | B | E | I | V | R | H | T | D | V | V | R | T | O | E |
| P | A | X | N | G | L | D | B | V | R | T | Y | Q | R | M |
| F | A | V | B | V | I | A | A | E | R | R | F | N | B | O |
| H | B | E | W | T | N | Y | S | O | U | P | L | O | A | D |
| K | W | C | S | D | K | R | W | M | L | P | F | V | I | R |
| N | U | I | E | H | K | E | C | S | D | N | A | B | H | V |
| Z | T | E | N | R | E | T | N | I | Y | V | W | G | C | T |
| E | A | O | Y | I | F | I | X | U | Z | X | T | O | E | T |
| Z | R | K | F | R | N | H | P | K | X | B | I | J | D | S |
| C | W | F | B | A | F | Y | T | R | J | L | V | W | R | A |
| V | D | J | Q | Y | W | D | W | B | O | E | O | T | N | N |

| BROADBAND | HYPERLINK | PAGES | UPLOAD |
|---|---|---|---|
| BROWSER | INTERNET | SERVER | WEB |
| DOWNLOAD | MODEM | SITE | |

Success for Schools: ICT – © Letts Educational 2003

Complete the table by filling in information about some internet service providers.

| Name of provider | Cost per month | Cost per call | Amount of web space offered | Number of email addresses allowed |
| --- | --- | --- | --- | --- |
|  |  |  |  |  |
|  |  |  |  |  |
|  |  |  |  |  |
|  |  |  |  |  |

**Unit 2 Publishing on the web**

Spend a few minutes looking at the simple website you have been given. Then try to answer the following questions.

**1** What is the title of the home page?

**2** How many pages are on the site?

**3** What are the titles of the other pages?

**4** How many links are on the home page?

**5** How many items are listed on the input devices page?

**6** On which page are VDUs found?

Here is part of the website showing links between pages. Complete the diagram by adding the other pages and links.

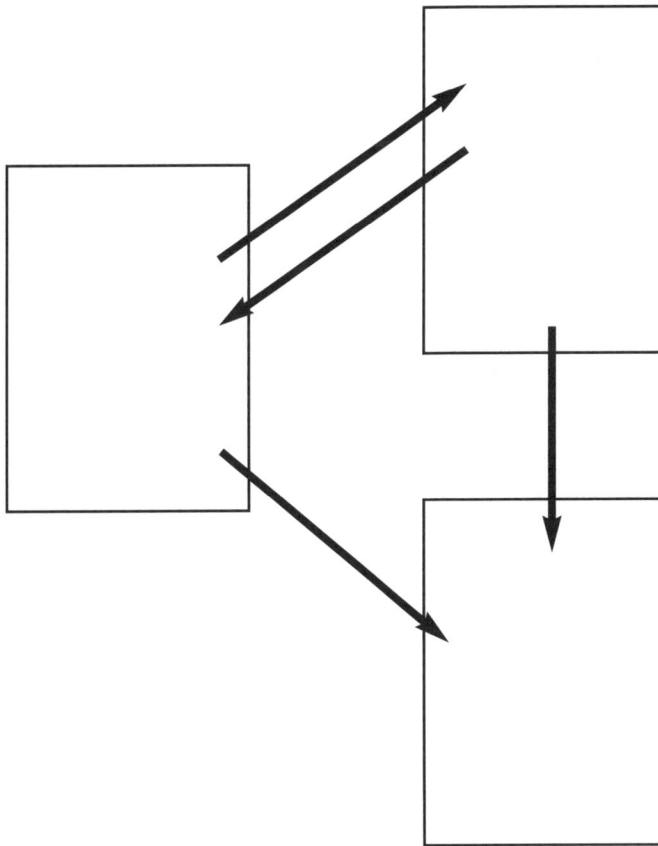

In this activity, you must describe the text on the screen below to your partner.
They must recreate the page as accurately as they can on paper.

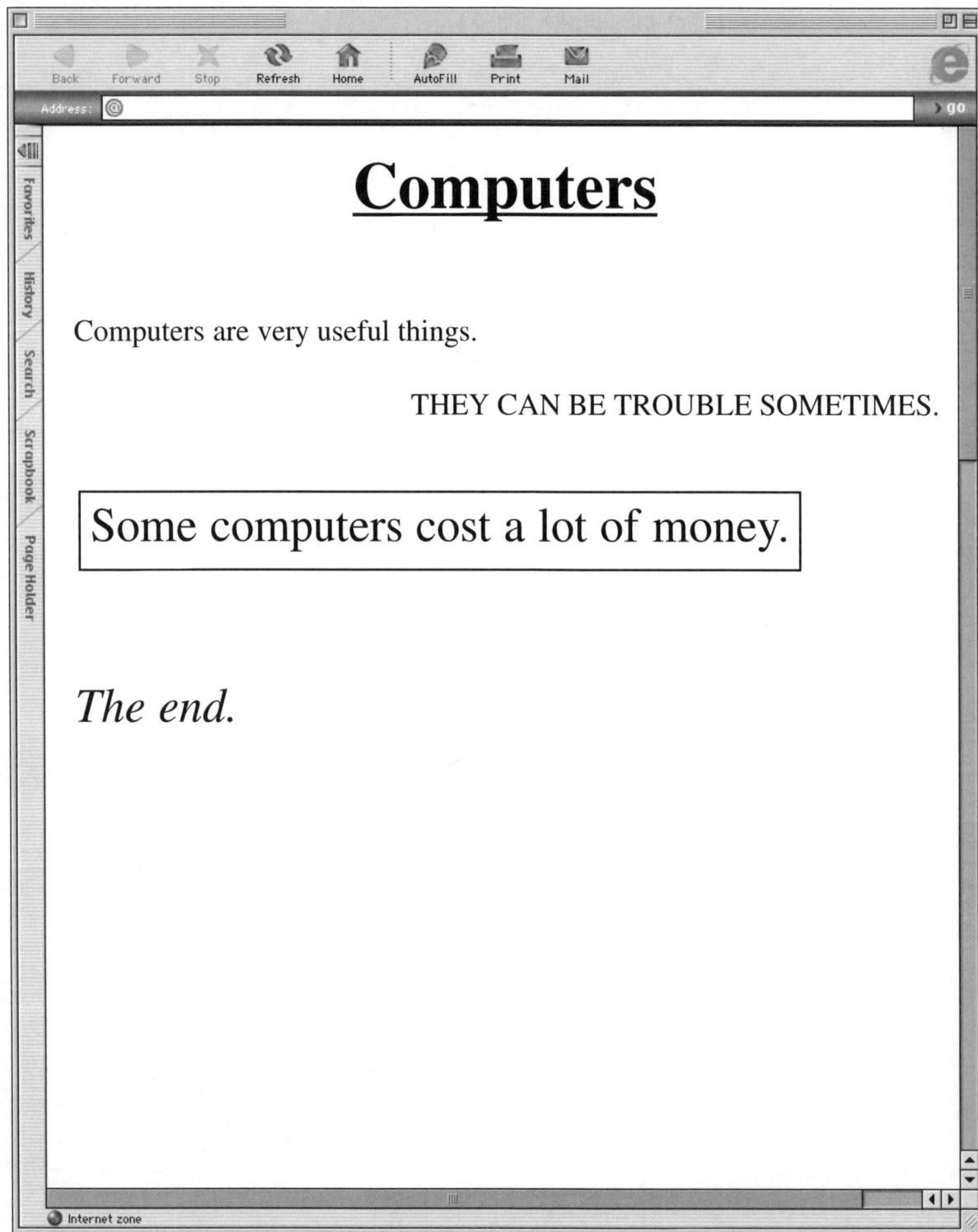

Back   Forward   Stop   Refresh   Home   AutoFill   Print   Mail

Address: @                                                         › go

Favorites   History   Search   Scrapbook   Page Holder

# Computers

Computers are very useful things.

THEY CAN BE TROUBLE SOMETIMES.

Some computers cost a lot of money.

*The end.*

Internet zone

Match the words on the left to their correct description.

| | |
|---|---|
| Headings | HTML has six levels of these |
| Link | The colour of the page behind the text |
| Background | An instruction to a web browser |
| White space | The area of a document with no text |
| Tag | A connection between pages |
| Text editor | Press this to update your screen display of a website |
| Editing | A program that can be used to change HTML |
| Refresh button | Call up something you have saved and make changes |

In this activity, you are going place another link on your 'Hello world' page. This time, you are going to link to a page of your own.

**Before you can have a link you need to set up a page to link to.**

1   **Load up your text editor.**

2   **Type in the following:**
    **<html>**
    **<body>**
    **This is page 2**
    **</body>**
    **</html>**

3   **Save the page using the name pagetwo.htm.**

4   **Load your 'Hello world' page in the editor.**

5   **Add the following line of code under the link to the BBC site you added earlier.**

    **<a href='pagetwo.htm'>My second page</a></p>**

6   **Save your page.**

7   **Reload your browser and try out your link.**

# 16 Crossword

Try to fit the words into the cells below.

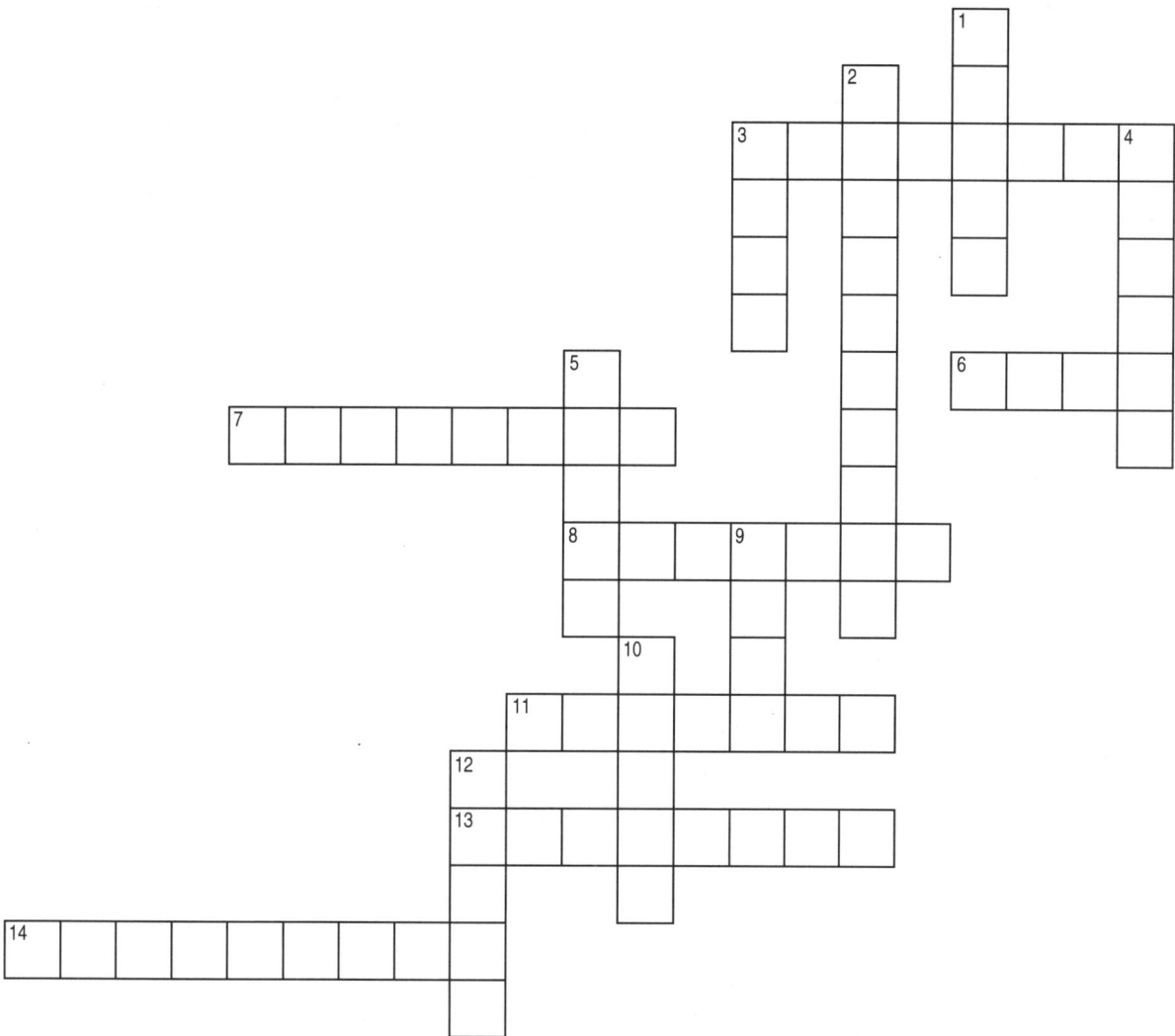

Browser          Links          Internet

Download         Background     Modem

Hyperlink        Tags           Pages

HTML             Headings       Server

Editing          White          Site

This activity is about making a simple map of a website. Read the description below and then try to complete the diagram showing the site map.

Jack has a website about himself and his family. It has 5 pages. The home page links to the 4 other pages. These pages are called, Myself, My Hobbies, My School and My family.

All the pages link back to the home page. The other pages link to each other by a link that says NEXT PAGE. The pages go round in the same order as the list above.

**Home page**

Success for Schools: ICT – © Letts Educational 2003

Look at all the mail you have collected. Count the number of items in each category and fill in the table below.

| | Mon | Tue | Wed | Thu | Fri | Sat |
|---|---|---|---|---|---|---|
| Advertising: Junk mail | | | | | | |
| Advertising: requested | | | | | | |
| Bills | | | | | | |
| Personal | | | | | | |
| Other | | | | | | |
| | | | | | | |
| | | | | | | |

Use this tally chart to record what types of organisations have your family's names and addresses. There are blank rows to include any others that you might see.

| Type of organisation | How many items |
|---|---|
| Bank | |
| Credit card company | |
| Insurance company | |
| Loan company | |
| Medical (hospital/doctor) | |
| Supermarket | |
| | |
| | |
| | |
| | |

| Data subjects | Reason for needing data |
|---|---|
| Staff including volunteers, agents, temporary and casual workers | |
| Suppliers | |
| Complainants, correspondents and enquirers | |
| Relatives, guardians and associates of the data subject | |
| Advisers, consultants and other professional experts | |
| Students and pupils | |

Success for Schools: ICT – © Letts Educational 2003

58 59

## Hardware

| Used by pupils | Used by teachers | Used by office staff |
|---|---|---|
| | | |
| | | |
| | | |

## Software

| Used by pupils | Used by teachers | Used by office staff |
|---|---|---|
| | | |
| | | |
| | | |

## Data or other

| Used by pupils | Used by teachers | Used by office staff |
|---|---|---|
| | | |
| | | |
| | | |

Unit 3 Data: use and misuse

| Problem | How it is dealt with | Who deals with it |
|---|---|---|
| Files might get lost if the server fails | | |
| Viruses might get into the network | | |
| The power might go off and files might be lost | | |
| New users need to be added | | |
| Someone forgets his or her password | | |
| Lots of non-essential material is being printed, wasting paper | | |

Enter the following information about your school.

**Name of school:**

**Name of Head Teacher:**

**Name of your ICT teacher:**

**Name of the town where the school is:**

**Number of computers in the computer room:**

**The word-processing software that you usually use:**

**The spreadsheet software that you usually use:**

|  | Input devices | Output devices | Connecting devices |
|---|---|---|---|
| The checkout |  |  |  |
| The back office |  |  |  |
| In between the checkout and the back office |  |  |  |

## Loyalty card application

### About You

(Fields marked * are required)

Your title: ▼

*Your first name or initial:

*Your surname:

*Address:

*Town:

County:

*Postcode:

E-mail: Please type this carefully.

Telephone number: Include STD code.

Are you? ○ Male ○ Female

Are you over 18? ○ Yes ○ No

### About Your Family

Number of children in your household under the age of 18:

Please give children's details. If you have more than two, please start with the youngest first.

| | Date of Birth (DD/MM/YYYY) | Gender | |
|---|---|---|---|
| **1st child** | | ○ Male | ○ Female |
| **2nd child** | | ○ Male | ○ Female |

We would like to offer our customers the best service possible and will, from time to time, conduct research. If you want to be contacted to participate in such research, please tick here, indicating which methods are acceptable to you.

☐ Telephone ☐ Direct mail ☐ E-mail

Success for Schools: ICT – © Letts Educational 2003

**Unit 3 Data: use and misuse**

These instructions are for Microsoft *Access*.

**1** Start *Access* and start a new blank database (make sure you click the radio button by blank *Access* database).

**2** Save it straight away as **sales** in your own folder.

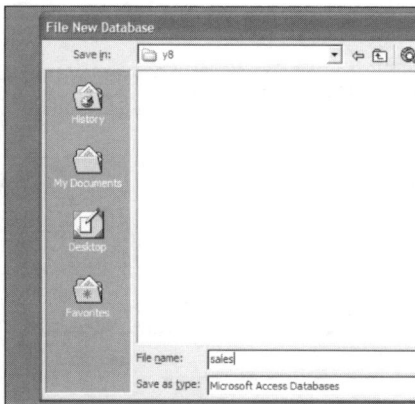

**3** Select **Create table in Design view**

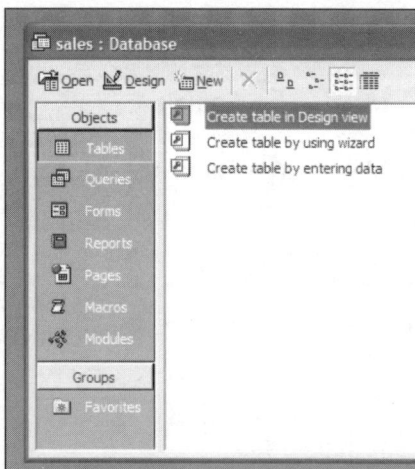

**4** Set up the fields.

**5** Save the table as **sales**. Say 'no' when it asks for a primary key.

**6** Go to datasheet view and enter the data. You will need a lot of data so you will have to swap till receipts with others.

**7** Aim to get at least 20 or 30 items typed into the database.

**8** When entering the data, make up card numbers, such as 1, 2 and 3. Use a different card number for each different till receipt that you use. The software will automatically save the data from time to time.

Success for Schools: ICT – © Letts Educational 2003

Find the database words in the grid. The words may go up, down or diagonally.

| H | Y | H | V | C | T | K | E | Y | Y | D | L | I | S | O |
|---|---|---|---|---|---|---|---|---|---|---|---|---|---|---|
| I | R | Q | Y | R | J | S | M | U | U | H | L | W | M | K |
| P | E | M | O | I | A | G | G | H | W | X | R | E | K | O |
| W | U | S | R | B | M | M | C | J | Q | H | E | Y | I | K |
| J | Q | B | A | N | U | M | E | R | I | C | P | F | H | F |
| T | T | T | X | S | V | I | Y | O | S | S | O | V | B | Z |
| S | A | E | S | Z | M | S | N | P | V | U | R | G | F | O |
| D | N | F | X | U | R | G | E | F | S | U | T | I | R | U |
| M | W | H | Q | T | F | J | B | A | V | E | L | X | I | N |
| Z | F | O | R | M | J | X | F | R | R | T | O | W | N | N |
| M | R | L | V | L | Q | J | U | Q | E | C | B | F | C | I |
| J | P | P | H | D | K | Z | W | R | N | B | H | R | Z | U |
| P | P | E | F | I | H | V | D | E | H | J | K | Y | J | G |
| E | L | B | A | T | M | A | O | R | L | Q | N | T | X | M |
| Q | B | Q | M | J | V | V | T | K | M | U | F | Y | I | O |

| DATABASE | FORM | REPORT | TABLE |
|---|---|---|---|
| FIELD | NUMERIC | SEARCH | TEXT |
| FILTER | QUERY | SORT | |

Unit 3 Data: use and misuse

Here is some data taken from a CSV file.

```
barcodenumber,description,make,quantity,price
2343434,beans,Heinz,4,0.49
2342344,spaghetti,HP,56,0.35
6646456,tomatoes,Napolina,54,0.3
```

**1** What is special about the first line?

**2** How much spaghetti is in stock?

**3** What is the selling price of a tin of beans?

**4** What is the barcodenumber for tomatoes?

**1** Load the file CSV 2

**2** Next, tidy it up.

**3** Highlight the whole sheet by clicking here:

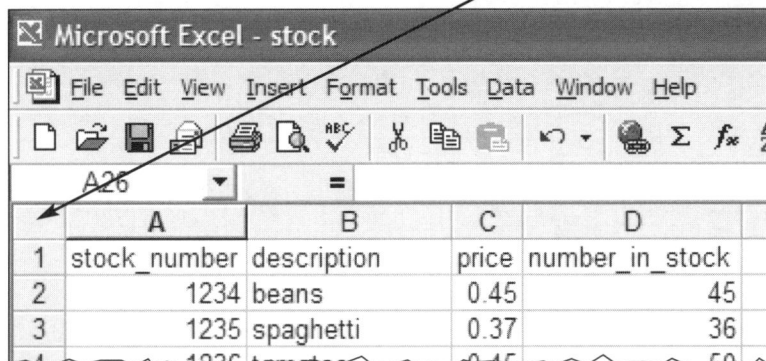

| | A | B | C | D |
|---|---|---|---|---|
| 1 | stock_number | description | price | number_in_stock |
| 2 | 1234 | beans | 0.45 | 45 |
| 3 | 1235 | spaghetti | 0.37 | 36 |

**4** Select **Format – Column – Autofit**.

**5** With the sheet still highlighted, select **Data – Sort**.

**6** Change the **Sort by** instruction to price. Leave the **Sort order** as ascending.

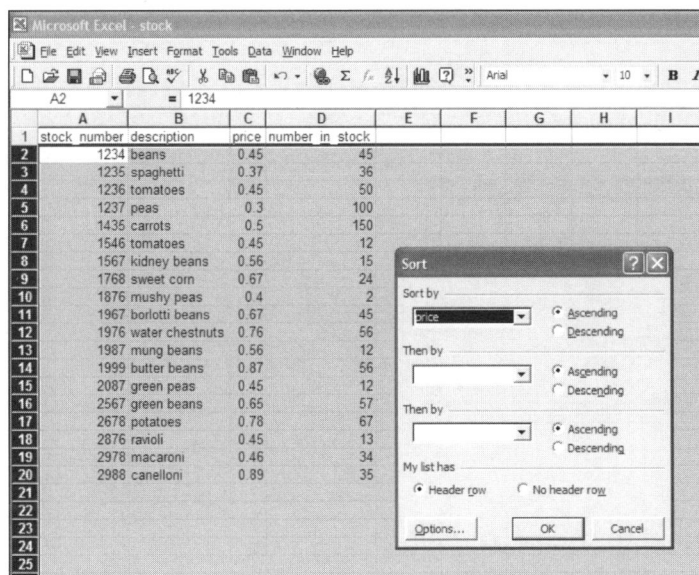

**7** Click OK.

**8** You will now be able to see which is the cheapest product.

## Further questions

**1** What is the most expensive item?

**2** Which item has the lowest stock?

**3** How many products begin with the letter "B"?

Unit 3 Data: use and misuse

**1** Highlight all the data.

**2** Select **Data – Filter – Autofilte**r.

**3** Notice that a drop-down box appears by each field name (column heading).

**4** Select the drop-down box next to **description**. Select **Custom**.

**5** In the dialogue box, choose **Begins with** and enter B in the box next to it.

**6** Click OK.

**7** Now select the drop-down box next to the **price** field.

**8** Choose **is less than** and enter .5

**9** When you click OK, you should see the answer you want.

**74**

These instructions apply to Microsoft *Access*.

**1** Start *Access* and start a new blank database (make sure you click the radio button by blank *Access* database).

**2** Save it straight away as **sales** in your own folder.

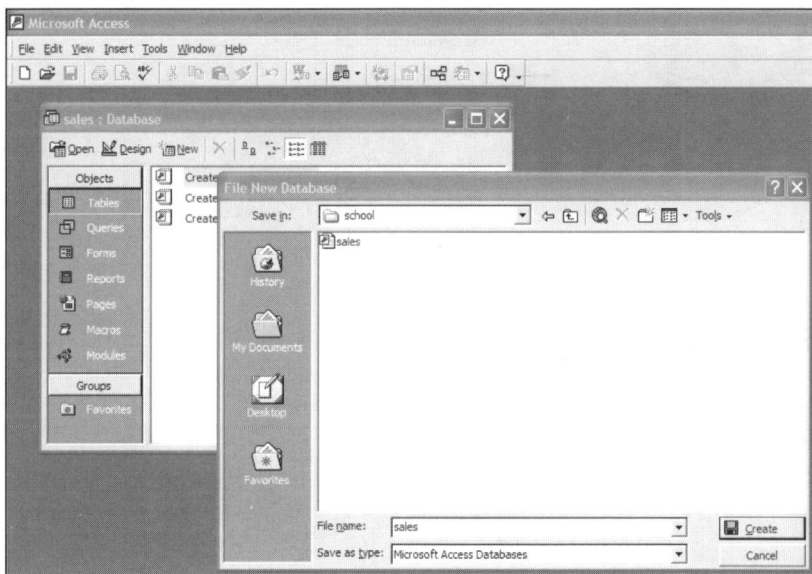

**3** There is no need to create a table for the data; Microsoft *Access* will do this for you. Go to **File – Get external data – Import**.

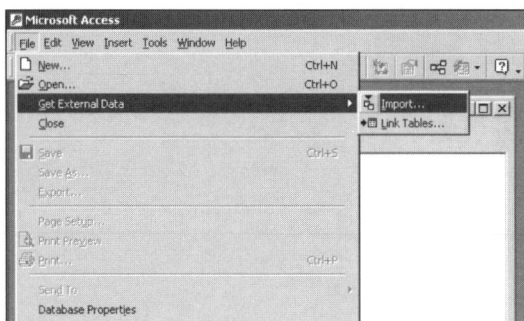

**4** Make sure you look for **Text files**. You are looking for file *CSV 3*.

**5** *Access* will recognise that the file is 'delimited' as it is a CSV file.

**6** Check the box that says **First row contains field names**.

**7** Let *Access* make a new table.

**8** Choose **stock_number** as a primary key.

Unit 3 Data: use and misuse

**1** Go to **Window – Sales: Database**.

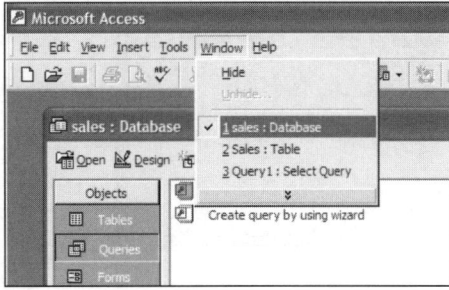

**2** Choose **Create query in Design view**.

**3** Add the **Sales** table.

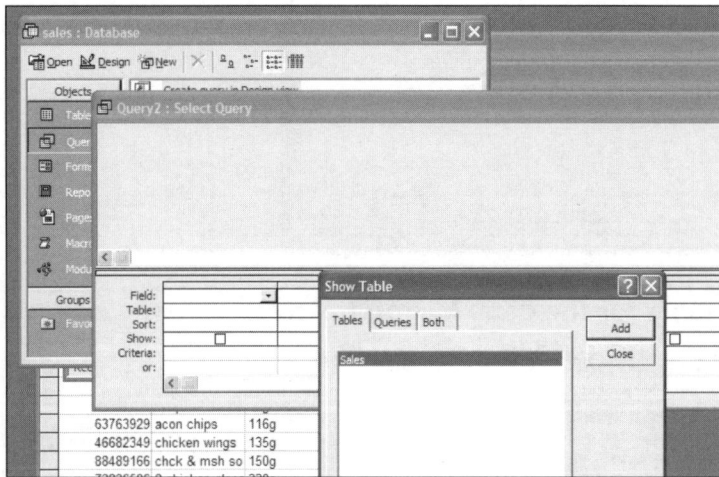

| | | |
|---|---|---|
| 63763929 | acon chips | 116g |
| 46682349 | chicken wings | 135g |
| 88489166 | chck & msh so | 150g |

**4** Add **Description** and **Price** to the query table by double clicking them.

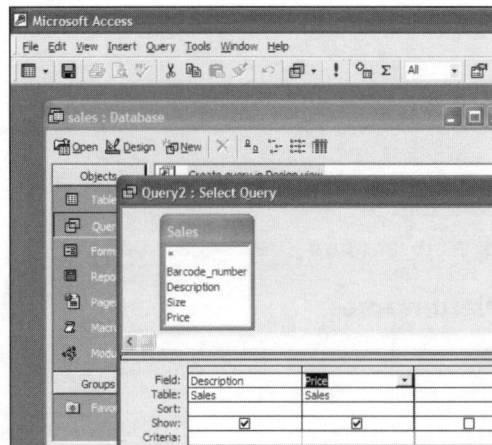

**5** Enter<.5 in the criteria box under **Price**.

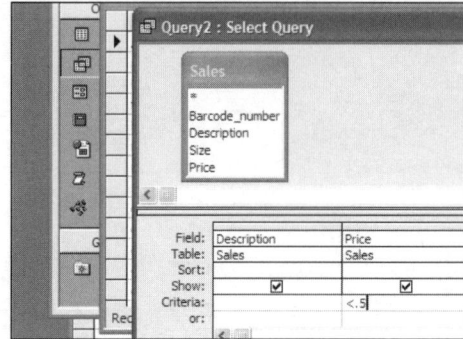

**6** Run the query by clicking the run button.

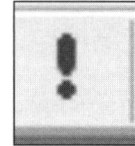

Success for Schools: ICT – © Letts Educational 2003

These are the main symbols you will need in making a system flow chart. Find out the meaning of each one and write it beneath the symbol.

Here's how to do it. Load your word-processor software. Make sure that the drawing toolbar is visible. If it is not, select it from **View – Toolbars – Drawing**. You will find flow chart symbols under AutoShapes.

Hover the mouse over the appropriate symbol. The tool tip feature will tell you what the symbol means.

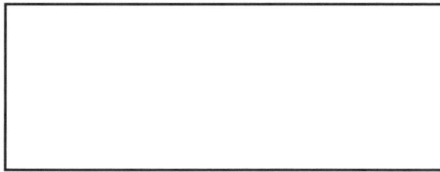

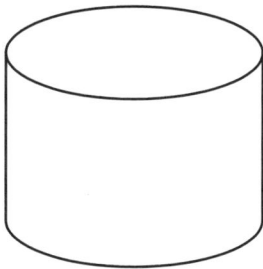

- Load the word-processing software
- Open the letter document
- Select **Tools** – **Mail merge** from the menu.
- Select **Create form letters** and press the **Active window** button.
- Select **Get data** – **Open data source**. Find the spreadsheet file called **CSV 4**.
- Select **Get entire spreadsheet**.
- You will then be asked to edit main document.
- Insert merge fields from the list that will be available on the menu.
- Lay them out neatly.
- Press the button – **Merge to new document**.

The top of the letter should end up looking something like this:

# Cheapo plc

**Anytown Industrial Estate
Anytown
AN6 &YG**

«Title» «Initial» «Surname»
«Address1»
«Address2»
«Postcode»

**Card Number: «Card_number»**

Dear «Forename»

Welcome to Cheapo's super loyalty card scheme. You are now able to collect points on everything that you purchase at any Cheapo store nationwide. As if that were not enough, you can get double points on many special promotions.

| F | Z | J | Q | E | D | R | S | Y | E | Y | G | M | U | P |
|---|---|---|---|---|---|---|---|---|---|---|---|---|---|---|
| C | P | B | C | I | W | B | A | E | W | V | I | Z | A | R |
| N | C | T | A | H | K | W | Y | L | R | E | Y | Y | D | O |
| H | I | L | T | P | B | J | Y | L | K | V | N | Y | M | U |
| N | U | S | V | H | I | N | K | D | Z | T | I | N | A | T |
| P | U | Q | W | G | K | X | V | F | H | E | F | C | I | E |
| R | X | Z | H | B | A | V | G | V | A | N | D | P | E | R |
| C | E | I | F | T | V | V | W | R | N | R | O | S | D | D |
| T | L | T | G | G | J | A | E | S | M | E | P | L | A | A |
| E | R | Z | U | M | E | D | O | M | J | T | J | K | B | S |
| X | L | I | D | P | I | N | G | Y | H | N | G | R | Z | J |
| Q | Z | G | F | V | M | F | B | Q | Q | I | R | Z | J | C |
| N | V | W | O | B | R | O | W | S | E | R | R | S | Q | R |
| D | C | R | O | P | F | I | C | R | H | N | U | L | S | E |
| C | P | X | K | C | P | X | L | J | D | N | Y | U | G | B |

**Unit 4 Information: reliability, validity and bias**

| BROWSER | HTTP | PROVIDER |
|---|---|---|
| COMPUTER | INTERNET | ROUTER |
| DIALUP | MODEM | SERVICE |

| Website address | Who put the website there? | Is the information balanced or biased? |
|---|---|---|
|  |  |  |
|  |  |  |
|  |  |  |
|  |  |  |
|  |  |  |
|  |  |  |
|  |  |  |
|  |  |  |
|  |  |  |

Activity
3

**7** Look for:

File type: Delimited
Separated by: Comma
First row contains field names

**8** Let it save it in a new table.

**9** Let Access add the primary key.

**10** Import to table Weather_data.

**1** Load MS Access.

**2** Select **Create new database.**

**3** Select **Create table in Design view.**

**4** Get external data – Import
Files of type: text files

**5** Find the file called CSV 5.

**6** The wizard will now guide you through the steps you
need to take.

Fill in the spaces in the boxes to give your opinions on each of these methods of communicating. Write in a score as indicated in the table. Remember that your audience is 10-year-olds.

| Method | Ease of setting it up<br><br>1: very easy<br>2: quite easy<br>3: quite difficult<br>4: very difficult | Effectiveness at getting the message across<br><br>1: very effective<br>2: quite effective<br>3: not very effective<br>4: very ineffective |
| --- | --- | --- |
| Text only | | |
| Text with graphics | | |
| Multimedia | | |
| A web page | | |
| A video | | |

Success for Schools: ICT – © Letts Educational 2003

These instructions are for use with Microsoft *Publisher*. They will need to be adapted for use with other DTP packages.

**1** You will need a graphic file and a long text file. Your teacher will tell you where to find them.
The graphic file is called *Image 3*.
The text file is called *Text 3*.

**2** Start your DTP software.
If the catalogue comes up, leave it by clicking **Exit Catalog**.

You will now have a new blank page.

**3** Click on the text frame tool.

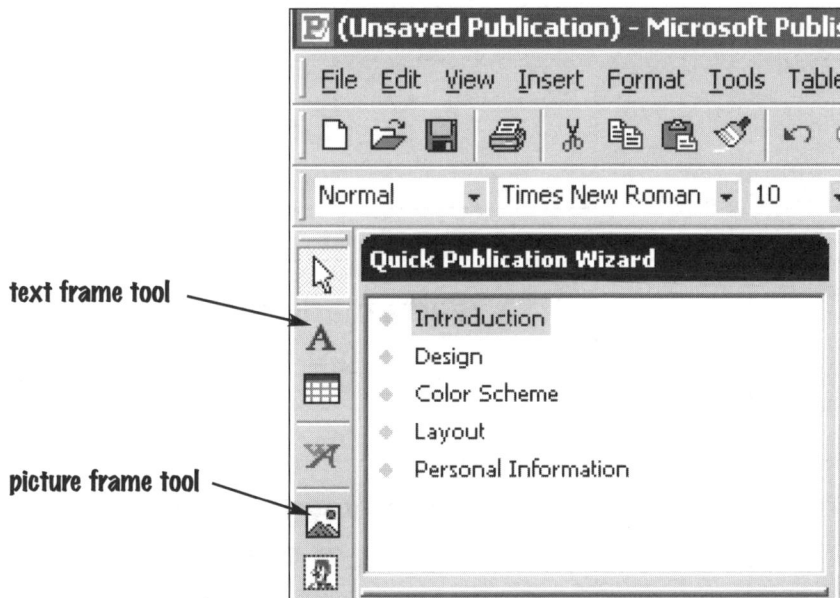

text frame tool

picture frame tool

**(Unsaved Publication) – Microsoft Publis**

File   Edit   View   Insert   Format   Tools   Table

Normal ▾   Times New Roman ▾   10 ▾

**Quick Publication Wizard**

◆ Introduction
◆ Design
◆ Color Scheme
◆ Layout
◆ Personal Information

**4** Draw out a rectangle to fill the page.

**5** Select **Insert Text File** from the menu.

**6** Navigate to the file *Text 3*.

**7** Double click on it.

You will be warned that it doesn't fit, so accept the suggestion that it will create extra space for it. If necessary, extra pages will be created.

Now we shall insert a graphic in the middle of the text.

**8** Click on the **Picture frame** tool and draw out a frame for the picture in the middle of the text. The text will readjust to accommodate the frame.

**9** Double click on the picture frame and select the graphic file *Image 3*.

Can you match the words on the right to the correct description?

| | |
|---|---|
| Cell | A set of buttons to click giving access commands |
| Toolbar | A horizontal set of cells |
| Formula | A single location in a spreadsheet |
| Row | A calculation in a cell |
| Sort | A ready-made instruction for doing a calculation |
| Save | An easy way to make a chart or graph |
| Function | Store a file on disc for future use |
| Column | Rearrange data into order |
| Chart wizard | The vertical sets of cells |

These layouts are to show what part of the spreadsheet might look like. These layouts can be improved on.

Here are screen shots of the actual cost sheet. One shows the layout, the other shows the formulae.

|  | A | B | C | D | E |
|---|---|---|---|---|---|
| 1 | | | Visits4Schools | | |
| 2 | **Venue cost** | | | | |
| 3 | Name of venue | Megaland | White Knuckle World | Water Ride Park | Rockworld |
| 4 | | | | | |
| 5 | Cost per person | £5.00 | £12.00 | £10.00 | £6.00 |
| 6 | Number of people | 59 | | | |
| 7 | | | | | |
| 8 | Total for venue | £295.00 | £0.00 | £0.00 | £0.00 |
| 9 | | | | | |
| 10 | | | | | |
| 11 | **Travel cost** | | | | |
| 12 | Coach size | 60 | | | |
| 13 | Coach per mile | £3.00 | | | |
| 14 | Distance travelled | 120 | | | |
| 15 | | | | | |
| 16 | Total for coach | £360.00 | | | |
| 17 | | | | | |
| 18 | | | | | |
| 19 | Total actual cost | £655.00 | | | |
| 20 | Profit | £98.25 | | | |
| 21 | | | | | |
| 22 | Cost to school | £753.25 | | | |
| 23 | | | | | |

|  | A | B | C | D | E |
|---|---|---|---|---|---|
| 1 | | | Visits4Schools | | |
| 2 | **Venue cost** | | | | |
| 3 | Name of venue | Megaland | White Knuckle World | Water Ride Park | Rockworld |
| 4 | | | | | |
| 5 | Cost per person | ='venue cost'!B1 | ='venue cost'!B2 | ='venue cost'!B3 | ='venue cost'!B4 |
| 6 | Number of people | 59 | | | |
| 7 | | | | | |
| 8 | Total for venue | =B5*B6 | =C5*C6 | =D5*D6 | =E5*E6 |
| 9 | | | | | |
| 10 | | | | | |
| 11 | **Travel cost** | | | | |
| 12 | Coach size | 60 | | | |
| 13 | Coach per mile | 3 | | | |
| 14 | Distance travelled | 120 | | | |
| 15 | | | | | |
| 16 | Total for coach | =B14*B13 | | | |
| 17 | | | | | |
| 18 | | | | | |
| 19 | Total actual cost | =B16+B8 | | | |
| 20 | Profit | =B19*15% | | | |
| 21 | | | | | |
| 22 | Cost to school | =B19+B20 | | | |
| 23 | | | | | |

The formula in cell E5 **='venue cost'!B4** refers to the contents of cell B4 on the venue costs sheet.

Here are two print outs from part of a spreadsheet which is used to produce quotations.

The first one shows the spreadsheet with the calculated values displayed.

| | A | B |
|---|---|---|
| 1 | | |
| 2 | **Venue cost** | |
| 3 | Name of venue | Megaland |
| 4 | | |
| 5 | Cost per person | £5.00 |
| 6 | Number of people | 59 |
| 7 | | |
| 8 | Total for venue | £295.00 |
| 9 | | |
| 10 | | |
| 11 | **Travel cost** | |
| 12 | Coach size | 60 |
| 13 | Coach per mile | £3.00 |
| 14 | Distance travelled | 120 |
| 15 | | |
| 16 | Total for coach | £180.00 |
| 17 | | |
| 18 | | |
| 19 | Total actual cost | £475.00 |
| 20 | Profit | £71.00 |
| 21 | | |
| 22 | Cost to school | £366.25 |
| 23 | | |

This one shows the formulae used. Find the mistakes and write the corrections in the space below.

| | A | B |
|---|---|---|
| 1 | | |
| 2 | **Venue cost** | |
| 3 | Name of venue | Megaland |
| 4 | | |
| 5 | Cost per person | ='venue cost'!B3 |
| 6 | Number of people | 59 |
| 7 | | |
| 8 | Total for venue | =B5*B6 |
| 9 | | |
| 10 | | |
| 11 | **Travel cost** | |
| 12 | Coach size | 60 |
| 13 | Coach per mile | 3 |
| 14 | Distance travelled | 120 |
| 15 | | |
| 16 | Total for coach | =B12*B13 |
| 17 | | |
| 18 | | |
| 19 | Total actual cost | =B16+B8 |
| 20 | Profit | =B19*15% |
| 21 | | |
| 22 | Cost to school | =B8+B20 |
| 23 | | |

Try to fit the words into the grid.

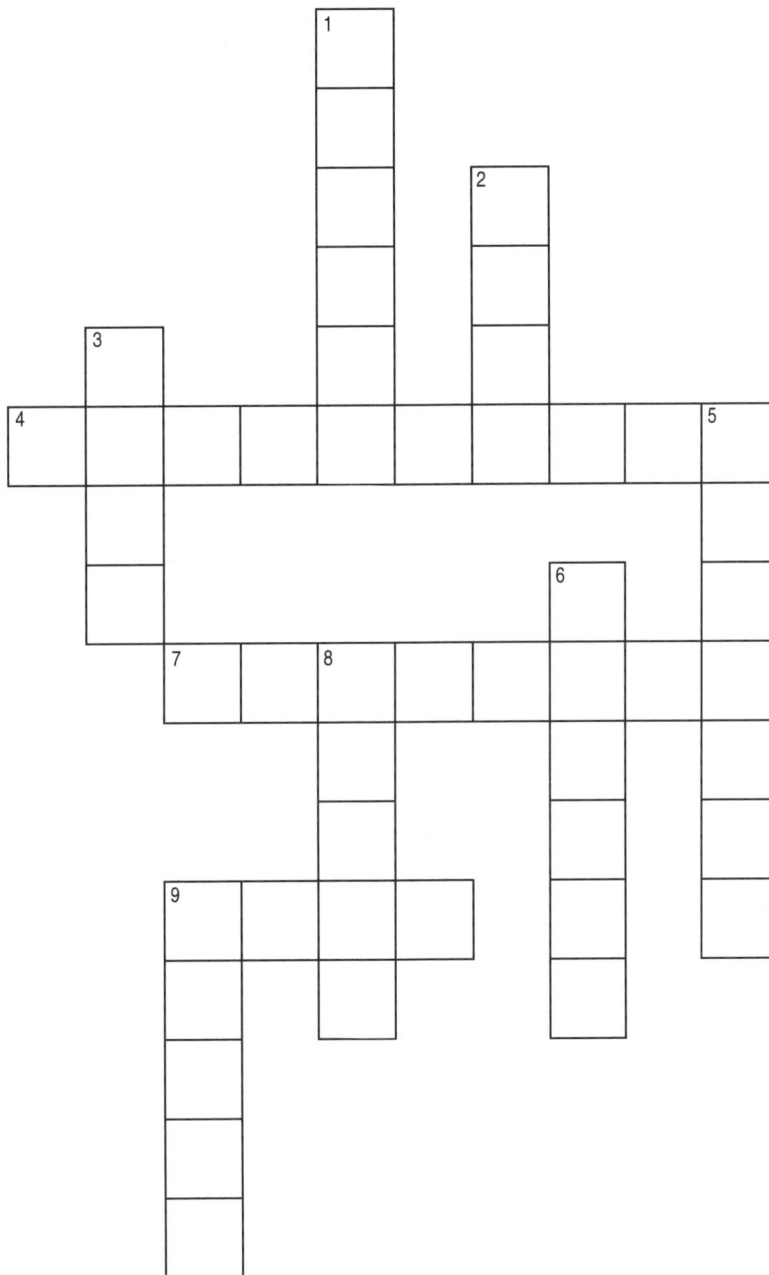

File

Field

Validation

Database

Table

Data

Text

Numeric

Backup

Record

Here is some data for you to start your database.

There is some space to make up and add some of your own data as well.

| School reference number | School name | Address 1 | Address 2 | Postcode | Contact | Booking made | Coach booked | Booking quote reference |
|---|---|---|---|---|---|---|---|---|
| 1234 | St Johns | Cobol Lane | Didsbury | DD3 3SW | Mr Dobbs | Yes | No | 4523 |
| 1235 | Anytown High | Window St | Anytown | AY1 6TP | Mr Fish | No | No | |
| 1236 | Matchville High | Tubbs Ave | Highville | HY7 2FT | Mr Singh | No | No | |
| 1237 | Hightown High | Peters Lane | Hightown | HT1 1WQ | Mr Peters | Yes | Yes | 5698 |
| 1238 | St Peters | Pascal St | Programville | PR2 5FG | Mr Jones | Yes | No | 4596 |
| 1239 | Jackson High | Devon St | Jackson | JK23 1QW | Mrs Jenkins | No | No | |
| 1240 | Phillips Grammar | Grammar School Lane | Oxtown | OT3 5TH | Miss Johns | No | No | |
| 1241 | Internet High | Router Rd | Surftown | SF4 5ED | Mr Betts | Yes | Yes | 6842 |
| 1242 | St Alberts | Albert St | Waterford | WE3 8UH | Mrs Perkins | No | No | |
| | | | | | | | | |
| | | | | | | | | |
| | | | | | | | | |
| | | | | | | | | |
| | | | | | | | | |

| X | L | D | R | Z | L | G | X | D | N | E | X | W | I | Z |
| C | V | C | X | R | C | O | R | P | O | R | A | T | E | F |
| T | I | F | O | R | P | E | G | U | M | O | E | G | H | I |
| U | F | L | J | Y | Y | A | P | O | C | T | A | B | U | U |
| F | W | S | I | L | W | S | M | K | X | C | S | H | V | S |
| I | N | X | F | M | Y | Y | I | T | J | E | E | C | R | D |
| T | Z | H | R | S | L | K | Y | I | I | V | P | L | F | G |
| I | D | A | T | A | H | O | Q | W | G | B | K | V | I | D |
| C | N | E | J | V | W | B | D | U | N | S | P | I | N | K |
| X | M | V | V | M | I | Z | I | H | L | J | H | G | A | G |
| I | O | G | O | Z | Y | K | W | E | L | S | O | N | N | R |
| Q | I | V | V | I | A | U | O | N | R | D | E | A | C | F |
| E | V | U | W | Y | C | J | U | O | J | Z | N | R | E | D |
| J | S | M | T | U | W | E | W | M | F | W | I | W | A | B |
| F | A | J | L | W | U | V | S | A | P | O | Y | P | G | S |

| BITMAP | DATA | FLYER | LOGO | SYSTEM |
|--------|------|-------|------|--------|
| CORPORATE | FINANCE | INVOICES | PROFIT | VECTOR |

Unit 5 Systems: integrating applications to find solutions

The company logo for *visits4schools* should appear on the itinerary as well as the name of the school that has booked the trip.

The itinerary then needs to clearly set out this information:

- The place
- The time of arrival
- The time of departure
- What is happening at the location e.g. Stop at service staion
- The total time from the start

Use this space to produce a draft outline for an itinerary.

Success for Schools: ICT – © Letts Educational 2003

Here is an itinerary for a school trip, which is a bit mixed up.
Can you put the events into the correct order?

| 19.30 | Leave London |
| 1.30 | Arrive at millennium eye |
| 7.30 | Leave school |
| 11.30 | Arrive in London |
| 7.15 | Assemble at school |
| 23.30 | Arrive at school |

Use this grid for your answer.

| | |
|---|---|
| | |
| | |
| | |
| | |
| | |

Now produce a draft itinerary for a school showing how this information will be displayed.

Unit 5 Systems: integrating applications to find solutions

Here are some simple rules for healthy use of a computer. Put the numbers on the diagram in the correct place.

1 Adjust your chair and VDU so that you are comfortable.

2 Your forearms should be approximately horizontal and your eyes the same level as the top of the VDU.

3 Arrange your VDU to avoid glare or reflections on the screen.

4 Have space under your desk to move your legs.

5 Adjust your keyboard so that you are comfortable.

6 Try to keep your wrists straight when keying.

7 Support your forearm on the desk

8 Do not grip the mouse too tightly.

9 Adjust the brightness and contrast accordingly.

10 Do not sit in the same position for long periods.

**Unit 5 Systems: integrating applications to find solutions**